THE COLLECTED POEMS OF BURNS SINGER

The Collected Poems of
BURNS SINGER

Edited and with an Introduction by
W. A. S. KEIR

Preface by
HUGH MacDIARMID

SECKER & WARBURG · LONDON

The collection *Still And All* was first
published by Martin Secker & Warburg in 1957

SBN: 436 46509 4

Printed in Great Britain by
Western Printing Services Ltd, Bristol

To the Critic

I have refrained
From trying to find
A law and order in poetry.
If you want rules
And styles and schools
Apply to the nearest côtery.

Acknowledgements

In addition to Dr Marie Singer and Dr Christopher Grieve (Hugh MacDiarmid), I wish particularly to thank Mr G. S. Fraser for editorial and other assistance, and Dr Eric D. S. Corner, Dr John Steele and Mr Jack Webster for invaluable biographical information.

Many of these poems have appeared in the following periodicals or anthologies:

Botteghe Oscure, Encounter, Lines Review, The Listener, New Poems 1955, Poetry Now (Faber), *Points, The Saltire Review, The Times Literary Supplement.*

A number have been broadcast on the Scottish Home or the Third Programme.

W.K.

Contents

Preface

I met James Burns Singer in Glasgow in the War years—the early
'40s. When I was introduced to him, I thought I was being 'had
on', because I could not believe the name was his real one, and
thought it designated a vocalist specializing in Burns songs, a
breed of which we have, or used to have (for things are changing) a
nimiety in Scotland. I soon learned different, however, and found
that here was a *rara avis* (probably the only one of his kind in all
'braid Scotland'). He was a torrential non-stop talker—but never
without having something to say well worth hearing, and evidence
of a quite unusually well-informed mind and a degree of in-
tellectual curiosity that seemed to have no bounds.

This was not a type who should have had the added misfortune
of growing up in Scotland, but he took it uncomplainingly, if not
in good part. At that time we had in Glasgow a new Arts Club
which attracted all manner of aspirants in literature and the other
arts. None of them, except Burns Singer, have come to anything
of the slightest consequence, but I thought at first that this Arts
Club might well come to rival one of those cafés in France or
Germany which proved foci and forcing-beds for so much of ultra-
modernist writing, painting, dancing, and music. Near by, not
associated with the Club, was a house which at that time accom-
modated W. S. Graham the poet, Helen Biggar the sculptor,
Robert Frame and Benny Crême, artists, and others, and it was with
this group, and one of their visitors, no less a person than Dylan
Thomas, that I came into closer contact with Burns Singer. Glas-
gow, of course, did not know that anything of this sort was
happening in its midst, and wouldn't have cared one iota if it had
known, unless the 'blue noses' in the population had heard of their
goings on and raised a typical puritanical brouhaha. About the
same time there was a hall in Scott Street where debates and
musical and dramatic evenings took place. This had been initiated
by David Archer, whose Parton Press had been the first publishers
of Dylan Thomas and other young poets. In all these places Burns
Singer was in his element, and I soon found that his range of
reading and stores of out-of-the-way information were quite
exceptionally extensive. In debates especially his volubility was

[xi]

overwhelming, and older members of the company were apt to resent so young a man knowing so much more than they could ever hope to know about practically every subject broached, and so ruthless in taking charge of the proceedings without the slightest deference to any of his elders who might be present (people like J. D. Ferguson, the painter and his wife, Margaret Morris, the dancer, or Andrew Taylor Elder, Donald Bain, George Hannah, 'Dick' Annand and other artists). In such company, Burns Singer was generally outstanding and often the very life of the party, though in addition to his adolescent presumption and unconcern for other people's feelings he had the drawback of being quite unable to 'suffer fools gladly'—or, indeed, at all—and never hesitated to say so.

I was greatly attracted by his breadth of reading, and of intellectual and aesthetic interests generally, and the way in which in a spate of argumentation he overrode everyone else I admired, because it betokened to me the immense drive I discerned in him— and hoped might be channelled into a worth-while course. At the same time I was apprehensive. He was very slightly built and did not look constitutionally strong (and here I do not mean in his inability to take much drink and not become a flaming nuisance as he frequently did). But I knew he had a bad background. His father was a wild and unaccountable character; his mother emitted a sort of desperate unhappiness, and finally committed suicide. Both were tremendously proud of Jimmie, and sure of his wonderful gifts, but I think without any real understanding of him. I had a flat in Glasgow near their home and young Singer formed a habit of dropping in on me and reading me huge swatches of poems of a kind which communicated nothing whatever to me. They went on and on, as though it were not words but ectoplasm that was coming out, swirling like a fog, wrapping me round in a cocoon. He had, of course, no regard whatever for any work I had in hand or any time-table I was obliged to work to. Finally my wife could not bear his time-consuming visits any more and locked the door of our garden which gave on to the lane by which he came. One night he found that door locked against him and for some reason was particularly determined to get in, so he started to climb the wall and had indeed surmounted it and was about to drop down on our side of it, when my wife espied him from our kitchen window. She was just in time to catch him as he came over, and seizing him by the seat of his trousers promptly threw him back over again.

That ended this imposition on my time, but I continued to meet him elsewhere on mutually convenient occasions and, not my 'cup of tea' at all though the juvenilia he had so monotonously read to me might be, there were already certain features of his writing I had noted which made me regret that I could not welcome his frequent intrusions. These features were: 1. his instinctive avoidance of the short lyric or anything song-like, of which in Scotland since Burns we have had an intolerable surfeit; 2. his tropism towards the long highly intellectual and even at times narrative poem; and 3. the complete originality of his work. There has been recently on the part of critics in various countries an impatience with or even dismissal of the English tradition in poetry. A recent critic, Nathaniel Tarn, has pointed out that the revolution in modern English language poetry is American: Eliot, Pound. 'Local post-Georgian poetry of validity is not English but Celtic: Yeats, Joyce, MacDiarmid, Dylan Thomas. A post-English reaction fades out after a praiseworthy but inconsequential brush with politics: Auden *et al*. Thomas, in whom Surrealism has its British day, provokes a new wave of little-Englandism. Rescue work on the English tradition: Hughes, Middleton, Silkin, Tomlinson, Redgrave, Macbeth, Wevill, however talented, or not, in its own terms, has not produced a new Poetics. The rest is beer and marital squabbles: politics at the level of the Profumo case.' And so on. Singer was free of all that. He had read everything all these poets had written, and was completely unaffected. His own life was wholly different. I must abandon the 'ectoplasm' comparison I made a little earlier. It was something even stranger than that, and not at all formless or lacking in development. It affected me as if someone were talking to me with great urgency in a language I did not understand—a language coming from whence I had no idea at all. It was clear that Singer and I were not on the same wave-length, and even now the poems in his only published volume, *Still and All* (Secker and Warburg, 1957) affect me as if they were spoken by a visitor from outer space—not a 'little green man' arriving from a flying saucer. There was nothing green about Singer at all. Nor did these poems present any of the barriers to understanding of much modern verse—recondite vocabulary, extreme allusiveness, purely private (personal) references of various kinds. On the contrary. 'Still waters

[xiii]

run deep'—Singer's poems had a full even flow of a depth I never fathomed, and came from a source I was quite unable to pin-point, That was not surprising. He was a rootless cosmopolitan. I was unable to identify and evaluate the various ethnic strands in his make-up. Well as I had got to know him by the middle of the '40s, I could never have predicted the sort of poetry he would create once he found his own voice. It is a voice quite unlike anything else in English poetry. The general effect reminds me of something I once said about the Scots language; 'There are words and phrases in the vernacular which thrill me with a sense of having been produced as a result of mental processes entirely different from my own and much more powerful. They embody observations of a kind which the modern mind makes with increasing difficulty and weakened effect.' It seems to me that something very similar must be said about Singer's poetry. It is all in plain, indeed in simple, English yet it is largely incomprehensible, abstruse in its subject matter if it has any other than the projection of a singular personality shorn of any of the circumstantiality of its everyday existence and delivered quintessentially and yet, utterly (almost inconceivably) alien though it is, put across with an incontestable conviction. This strange tide of expression is nevertheless in his best and most inscrutable poems under his complete control, as is shown by the way in which every now and again, with superb gnomic force, he makes clinching statements of a most challenging and unchallengeable kind; e.g. 'He made love perfect though he left it mourning' or, again, 'O do not watch. Their lack of loveliness will set you sobbing' or, once more (from 'Advice To A Young Lady'):

> Alone at bedtime you diminish still
> And harden to defend what grows more small
>   With each defence until
>   There's nothing left to fall.

Many of his verses resemble Melchizidek in being 'without ancestry or progeny'. Taken in conjunction with his enormous reading, and the range of his interests, the lack of relationship to other poets in his work is very remarkable.

Though there is little of it in any of his poems he was not incapable of the sharpest particularity and if a test is sought to show the great potentiality that his early death left unrealised, that can perhaps be best, or at any rate, most easily found, by comparing

[xiv]

two poems on not unrelated themes which appear side by side in John Holloway's anthology, *Poems of the Mid-Century* (Harrap, 1957). These are W. S. Graham's well-known 'The Nightfishing', and Burns Singer's 'S.O.S. Lifescene'.

> What matters is the cry, the cry like a screw,
> Sharp-oiled to turning, clean-cutting fish-silver through
> And through the teak air,
> A makeshift repetitive batter to riveting prayer.
> Like stitching sails this windfall patches men,
> Question to answer in a great bear-hug,
> Thick-fibred needlework, an electric plug,
> Nine cock-crows savage the air and cry us all home.

There Singer was writing of something of which he had vital first-hand experience. For after all in listing the things that even at the onset struck me about his poetry, I omitted perhaps the main one. His concern with the sciences. Not for him Lord Snow's 'Two Cultures'. Still less the peppering of his verses with a few words like 'pylons' or 'locomotives' to seem up-to-date and with-it.

> A blankness numb as a star, and, like a star
> In stillness, is not still through lack of motion
> But because of the unmoving distance
> Cannot move, or seem to move, is pasted
> Millions of years of light away in rotation
> That's faster than ours, is held there, still as a star.

Whatever importance I may attach to Singer's poetry—or, still more, to the poetry I feel sure he would have written if he had lived—I attach far more to the loss as it seems to me of something Scotland completely lacks and needs above all—a great critic. Critics in Scotland are rare as snakes in Iceland. As Dr John Holloway (to whom, when Dr Holloway was a lecturer in Aberdeen, I feel sure Singer owed a subtle, unimitative, but profound debt—or was it merely some kinship of mind?) has said, most of what purports to be literary criticism is nothing of the kind but merely personalia. Many scores of articles have been written in the last six years in this country, in America, and in many European countries, about my own poetry—many of them excellently written, extremely interesting, and even very flattering—but almost none of them appertaining at all to real literary criticism.

Burns Singer's long essay on my work (absurdly entitled 'Scarlet Eminence: Hugh MacDiarmid') which appeared in *Encounter* (March 1957—i.e. five years before the sudden outburst of writing about me which coincided with my seventieth birthday) is an exception. It is a brilliant piece of work. On the surface, one would have thought that Singer was about the last man to understand and sympathise with what I had done. As a rule I am condemned for expressing at one and the same time incompatible views on all sorts of subjects, and in particular writers about me almost invariably find that I am a 'queer sort of Communist' and doubt whether 'my views could be acceptable to the Kremlin' (though as a matter of fact I have documents showing that they are, and that they have also been wholeheartedly endorsed by the Writers' Unions in Czechoslovakia, Italy, and elsewhere). It never occurs to such writers that what they think is wrong with my Communism is in fact due to wrong ideas of what Communism is on their own part.

About my contradictions and inconsistencies, Singer's quality as a critic was shown in this wonderful essay by such a statement as this: 'The spiritual dogmatist is thus confronted by ten thousand heresies, but for the poet they are so many truths and the unique absurdity of the situation increases that number to ten thousand and one. I say "for the poet" because the poet's method of expression is a technique for discovering these truths at the point of their appearance within himself, before they have had time to fossilise into ideologies: he can express them when they are no more than a particular movement of his blood, before they have reached the stage where he can decide whether or not to believe in them. It was a plethora of such truths, instinct within himself, that Mac-Diarmid uncovered, revelation by revelation, in the eight main symbols of the *Drunk Man*. It is because they were each emotively present in him and each could be arrived at only after the other had been realised that his poem has the perfectly organic quality of an evolutionary sequence in biology. No matter how accidental his sudden transitions from one mood to another may seem when they are observed in isolation, they are, the genetic mutations, regulated by the fact that any accident other than the one which happened would have led to a very different result, and, probably, to a dead end. The total pattern thus acquires the aspect of inevitability which makes it, for those who understand its language, a very readable and satisfying poem.'

Having regard for Singer's age that is a very remarkable perception and is enough in itself to attest his critical capacity. His youth—and, despite his immense reading, the fact that he had never read Lukacz, Adorni, Benjamin, or, most important of all, Gramsci—excuses his absurd idea that 'His [my] Communism is not a simple matter of more pay for the workers and more jobs for the boys, but a genuine ascetic religion. By forcing society to organise itself more efficiently, much energy that is at present wasted could be diverted to one task that is truly human, that of understanding, to the point of despair and beyond it, the actual extent of what is understandable and thus to a sophisticated acceptance of those mysteries which cannot be understood. Such an attitude towards Communism could hardly have been more acceptable to Comrade Stalin than Pound's opinions to Herr Hitler.'

Space does not permit me to go further into this great question here, but if it did I could illustrate from Singer's own subsequent writings his steady growth in knowledge and understanding. Much of his critical writing was contributed (unidentifiably because anonymously) to *The Times Literary Supplement*, but I believed that it was he who wrote a very remarkable full page article about my work in *The Times Literary Supplement* of 31st December, 1964 (i.e. it did not appear until after Singer's death which occurred, when he was only thirty-six, in September 1964). Here it is stated in terms which I fully accept (and which have no parallel in writings about me save in certain passages of the above-mentioned *Encounter* essay of Singer's) that: 'Mr MacDiarmid hates humanitarianism so much that he will not even call himself a humanist. In his memorable contribution to the Oxford Union debate he denounced a prevailing Western morality of endaimoniam with a faint Christian colouring; it was like a breath of chilly air, and most of his hearers must have shivered and reflected that such a humane and generous, if too cosy, morality was after all their own. . . . MacDiarmid's heroes, like Lenin, are men of iron hardness. . . . Compassion for human suffering, though he has suffered much and is deeply aware of suffering, is not the motive behind either his nationalism or his communism. Behind his nationalism there is the wish to bring a submerged and thwarted culture, an Ur-Gaelic culture, to full flowering. Behind his communism there is a wish to bring about, or help to bring about, an evolutionary mutation, a radical transformation in the human psyche.'

I understand now that it was not Singer who wrote these sentences. If he did not then he certainly, towards the end, could and should; and if he did not, then I cannot think of anyone else, writing in the English language, who could. Certainly whoever other than Singer himself wrote them must have read, and profited by, Singer's quite exceptional *Encounter* article, and it took a first-class man to do that. That, I think, is the measure of the critic who perished before his work was done in the tragically early demise of Burns Singer.

HUGH MACDIARMID

Introduction

The work of some writers requires little or no introduction. Burns
Singer, however, was such a very unusual and complex person that
some knowledge of his life and background is essential. He was by
birth a mixture of many races. His childhood and youth, and a
great part of his short adult life, were unsettled to an extreme. He
was a cosmopolitan who was basically at home nowhere. He was
a poet and also a scientist. He loved simplicities, yet his mind
was continually being tempted in Coleridgean manner by all kinds
of abstruse and abstract speculations. He was an excellent literary
critic of wide and acute sympathies, but he tended to dismiss even
his finest articles and reviews as the merest hack journalism. He
spoke equally disparagingly about his book on the sea and the
fishing industry, *Living Silver*, but he was delighted when it was
praised by fellow-scientists. Even his appearance and his manner
were out of the ordinary. Slightly built and with a shock of blond
hair, he gave the impression of an electric energy and of a hard
physical and intellectual angularity, and torrents of talk would
alternate with periods of withdrawal and silence. And above all he
was completely original. But this meant that he was odd man out
from the very beginning, a displaced person in the fullest sense, and
his social behaviour varied from the very arrogant or the very gentle
to the deliberately outrageous. And this meant also that he was
not very often the easiest or most relaxing of company. He could
be gay, he nearly always was stimulating, but one felt that a pro-
found despair was not very far below the surface. Indeed through-
out nearly all his life, even during the last few years when he was
married, otherwise the happiest period he knew, he suffered from
persistent and recurring melancholia, and several times, soberly
and dispassionately, he contemplated suicide, and on at least one
occasion attempted it. 'He is a man capable of suffering,' Norman
McCaig said of him in a B.B.C. broadcast in 1957—'born to
suffer, one might think.' And this was felt by many others far less
acute than Mr McCaig, a fellow poet who also knew him per-
sonally, for he gave almost everyone he met the impression not
only of a remarkably penetrating intelligence and intensely sensi-
tive feelings, but of having his nerve-ends exposed to the world,

[xix]

raw and unprotected. Thus in one sense much of his life, and much of his work, was a search for identity. In another, although throughout he experienced a great deal of both inner and outer turmoil, what he longed for above all was some equivalent of T. S. Eliot's 'still point of the turning world'. *Still and All* was not chosen casually as the title of the only volume of poems published in his lifetime. I remember him discussing it with me, indeed lingering over its many implications, three years before the collection appeared in 1957.

Many of Burns Singer's characteristics and problems, then, were inherited and conditioned by the circumstances of his birth and upbringing, and he himself left several brief autobiographical sketches, published and unpublished. One of these appeared in *Encounter*, March 1957, along with his essay on Hugh MacDiarmid, and I give the essential part here:

> Born in 1928, a New York mongrel, I was brought to Scotland as a young child, and there educated. Two terms were enough to convince me that a full course of Eng. Lit. at Glasgow University would kill my interest in English Literature and cripple whatever talent might then have been mine. So I left Scotland for London where, at the age of seventeen, I found myself teaching mathematics to helpless adolescents at a dubious private school. The headmaster died of a heart attack, perhaps precipitated by my incompetence, and I fled to Cornwall where I lived in a tent and was lucky enough to come under the tutelage of W. S. Graham. Two years in Europe followed. The paternal interest of the painter Wols is all I care to recall of this miserable period. On return to Glasgow I took up Zoology because, as I told the master of studies, I wanted to 'write poems about animals'. From there to Aberdeen as a very junior member of the Scottish Home Department's Marine Laboratory, a job I was able to stick for four years because it involved considerable periods at sea. In the end, however, even they couldn't compensate for the demoralisation I suffered ashore. Therefore to London where, during the past sixteen months, I have been writing unsteadily but, looking back on it, very plentifully.

This I have quoted because it says, obviously, what Burns Singer—or Jimmy as he was always known—wished at that time to isolate in a brief summary of his career up to that date. Some of the statements here, however, are further elaborated, and indeed given a slightly different emphasis, in the rough draft of an unpublished sketch written a year later. There, for example, he expands on his earliest years as follows:

> I was born in New York City, 29th August, 1928, of very mixed parentage (Polish, Jewish, Irish etc.) and spent my infancy in the back of a car or on a ship as my parents travelled about. (My father was a salesman.) When I was four I was brought to Scotland and my education commenced. . . .

He also makes it clear that his meeting with W. S. Graham, a poet whom then as later he much admired, was far from a matter of luck, and that he deliberately sought him out:

> I acquired a little money and went to Cornwall to further my studies in verse composition under the tutelage of W. S. Graham. I found him living in a caravan; so I bought a tent and parked it in the next field.

And he also gives fuller details of his journeys abroad, and fuller and more serious reasons for returning to Glasgow and the university:

> After a visit to my parents in Glasgow, I went to Paris, ostensibly to join the American Army. [He was, of course, and remained till his death, an American citizen.] Luckily they chucked me out after a fight with an anti-Semite. . . . In Paris, however, I was lucky enough to come under the influence of the painter Wols. Ever since I have refused to fight anybody. Back to Glasgow where the chief influence was that of Hugh MacDiarmid, who still seems to me the greatest poet alive, with the possible exception of Ezra Pound—and even that is scarcely possible. His were many of the reasons [sic— this is a draft only] that decided me to study Zoology and I was very fortunate in finding, at Glasgow, the greatest living authority on Phylum Mollusca, in the person of Professor C. M. Yonge, C.B.E., F.R.S., to whom I owe whatever little I know about animals. He, like Graham, like Wols, like MacDiarmid, is (in the case of Wols, unhappily, was) a great

teacher. I was very lucky to know such men. I did not complete my degree course. The death of my mother and the illness of my father forced me to get a job—in Aberdeen as a Marine Scientific Assistant. It finally bored me—after four years. So I came to London.

There are still some obvious omissions, however, in both these accounts, which in any case take us up only to 1955, when he left Aberdeen, and to the beginning of his stay in London, and in addition some of the information is camouflaged or slanted. The following is a more complete though still inadequate account of his life, and one which I have deliberately kept as factual as possible. It would be only too easy to indulge in amateur psychological speculation—a temptation I have preferred to resist—and in any case for once at least the facts speak adequately for themselves.

'Born in 1928, a New York mongrel . . .' is our starting point. Jimmy did not speak much of his past but when he did it was usually in such terms, sometimes with sardonic amusement, sometimes with detached scientific curiosity, and only rarely with bitterness. In fact he usually understated rather then overstated, and would speak apparently casually of events which could easily have lent themselves to dramatisation. His ancestry, for example, was even more complicated than this phrase suggests. His father, Michael Singer, was born in Manchester, a second generation Polish-Jewish immigrant to England who later emigrated to the United States. His mother—Michael Singer's second wife, the first having died in childbirth—was Bertha Burns, and she was born in Greenock in Scotland of Irish, Scottish, and Norwegian extraction. He himself was given the names James Hyman Singer, and he had one elder half-sister by his father's first marriage, and one younger brother, Myer. Further, his father was not only a salesman, but a failed salesman—it was one such failure out of many which brought the family back to Scotland—often ill, nearly always poor, unstable and neurotic, and never lasting long in any one job. The fact that his father kept on hoping against all the evidence, with a kind of resigned desperation, that things would somehow miraculously improve, the fact that he developed a very genuine and totally uncomprehending admiration for Jimmy's potential, and the fact that his mother did her utmost to hold the family together and protect it from what she considered contamination by the worst elements of Glasgow, (vide his article, 'Glasgow', *The Saltire Review*, Spring 1955), cannot disguise for a moment that the whole background of his early years was of nagging insecurity and poverty, of family tensions and family neuroses and unhappiness. Meanwhile he began school, already showing precocity and already being considered by his schoolfellows as an oddity, and as such treated far from sympathetically. And very soon, as he himself tells us in a note to *The Poetry Book Society Bulletin*, February 1957, he had begun, at the age of six, to write. But in any case after seven years near and in Glasgow he was again on the move, being evacuated at the very beginning of the second world war, because of the fear of the bombing of Clydeside, along with his brother Myer. He was sent to Maud, a village in Aberdeenshire, and Mr Jack Webster, now a journalist, has recalled his arrival, the atmosphere of the period, and something of the time he spent there:

> I first met him on that grey morning of September 2, 1939. The war was upon us and as an eight-year-old I had stood at the railway station that morning waving goodbye to the Terriers—all Gordon Highlanders—as they stuffed whisky gills into their hip pockets and boarded the train for God-knows-where.
>
> In the afternoon I was back at the station for an incoming train, the load of Glasgow evacuees who were coming to the safety of the countryside. . . . They were marched in a crocodile to the Victoria Hall where they were allocated to homes in the village and surrounding farms. We had room for two—and they turned out to be James Hyman Singer and his brother, Myer Singer—and soon they settled in as my adopted brothers, me being an only child.
>
> Myer was worldly and perky, the first child I had ever seen wearing a proper sailor's suit (on Sundays). Jimmy was quiet and unlike other boys. He was studious, mild-mannered, but capable of chalk-white tempers when his patience was tried.
>
> Most of the children went wild in their new-found freedom of the countryside . . . but he remained quiet, and, to most of us, a bit of a mystery. At Maud school, however, he found a kindred spirit and firm friend in the person of Miss Cameron, the Latin and English teacher. . . . She was possibly the first

person to detect the genius of Jimmy Singer. She guided and encouraged him and, while few others were capable of seeing anything in him apart from oddness, she would say 'this laddie will go far.'

Unfortunately this original arrangement at Maud lasted only a short time. Mrs Webster, to whom Jimmy had already become attached, was taken ill, and he and Myer had to be removed to the local Parish Home, or 'Poorhouse', as it was known, a grim, forbidding-looking building, and though their stay there was brief—another kindly family, the Rothneys, took them in—this further transition, the way Jimmy felt he was being pushed around like a piece of lost luggage, naturally added to his already considerable feeling of isolation and indeed alienation. For already the pattern is becoming even clearer than before, as Jack Webster shows in his account of a visit to Maud by Jimmy's parents in the first winter of the war:

> My mother remarked to Mrs Singer about Myer being a cheery, likeable lad, but Mrs Singer replied in terms which showed clearly where her affections lay. Jimmy was the gentle one, the apple of her eye. My mother felt that Jimmy was likely to be a worry.

Fear that Jimmy was likely to be a worry was to become a refrain.

In 1943 Jimmy was back at school in Glasgow, and he began, then aged fifteen, to keep a regular diary, where he recorded his day to day life at home and at school, his relationships with his family, friends and schoolmasters, his wide reading, his already original views on literature quite irrespective of established opinion and fashion, and his own experiments in writing both poetry and prose. There is nothing whatsoever unusual in this in itself, of course, but in some respects this diary is a revealing and startling document. His first entry, for example, begins 'I write in good health were it not for an uncouth pain in my eyes which marauds my brain. . .' This, like some of the other entries, is rather self-conscious, and is partly written for effect—if only on himself—but already he is fairly acute in analysing his own problems. He fully realises that there is 'a mad, convulsive, neurotic, melancholic, introspective' side to his character. He realises too that he suffers from a 'baffled conceit'. And he questions himself: 'I am either

[xxiv]

a genius or a fool. Which is it? But my premises are false. . . . Perhaps there is something else at bottom, my arrogance.' And he can also be objective about his family—one feels that he has been forced to be objective—and when his failure of a father and his equally pathetic friends pontificate in their dreary Glasgow back street about 'big business and Capital' he records that he was 'hard put to it to keep from laughing outright. It was all immensely moving and comical, philosophical and gross.' Then on the darker side, apart from his mother's almost permanent depression, there was also an aunt who stayed with them from time to time, and who twice attempted suicide. And it was Jimmy, still only fifteen, who apparently insisted that a psychiatrist be consulted, and who seems to have conducted most of the initial interviews. But more to the immediate point are frequent entries beginning 'Wrote eighteen pages today'—or twenty, or sixteen—these often appearing alongside another recurring entry, 'All as always.' There are also two revealing postscripts added two years later, in 1945. The first refers to a long poem called *The Crossroads*, which, like a novel he, attempted, seems to have disappeared:

> Today I typed *The Crossroads*. Nothing but zero, counted and numbered on the disappearing page which grows as black as hate. . . Nothing but nothing. [Here follows a whole line of 'Os'] My metres are faulty because I attempt too much. I want to revolutionise the whole appearance of English poetry, to make it roll through a dozen accented syllables and skim a dozen unaccented. God! Give me patience to bear myself or courage to destroy myself.

In the second postscript he had been reading a critic, presumably D. S. Savage, on D. H. Lawrence:

> I have just been reading Savage on Lawrence. I am infuriated. I will not go with S. into the chasm of good or bad, nor with Lawrence into his cell of NOW. Nothing is real but what is, that is eternal. I deny mankind. Society is an illusion, a mask men put on to hide themselves. . . . What do I assert? I assert men. . . . and above all I assert myself. I am.

But the most striking entry in this diary was written not by Jimmy but by his mother. I have naturally considered carefully whether to publish this, particularly in view of subsequent events, but I have decided to do so partly because of the wish she herself expresses in the second paragraph, partly because it throws an essential light on their relationship and was preserved by Jimmy himself, and partly because it is a moving human document written by a very unhappy woman. It consists of only two pages one of which is slightly torn, and I have inserted certain words in brackets where the sense is obvious, leaving larger missing parts blank. It is headed simply 'This Happened':

What could be more fitting than to write my life story on the opposite page of my eldest son's journal as he sees fit to call it who has given up all I have striven and suffered to put him where he has all his life wanted to be.

I should like any readers if ever this gets into any other hands to read it carefully and remember each part and each word is the truth, the whole truth and nothing but the truth.

I am not a good English scholar and there will probably be lots of errors, but remember I have only been in school till the age of fourteen years, and those days the classes were larger and the teachers had no time for slow learners.

My father was born in Ireland, but came to Scotland with his parents at the age of nine. My mother was of Norwegian birth, but born in this country.

They were married at an early age and had very little of this world's goods in fact rather poor. What they lacked in money they made up in children, there was eleven of a family, nine girls and two boys.

[My] memory goes back to a very early age and I can remember as a very young child being rather anxious [about] everything I saw around me. It used to . . . . . . to see my dad and my two oldest . . . . . . to go out to the factory, these days work started at 6 A.M. After they would leave the house I clearly remember crying and being asked what was wrong, but I never answered. I just kept on crying. Then at night when they all got home my dad used to go out . . . . . . and each night there was a quarrel when he got back but I could never understand what it was about and it does not really matter in this book.

When I was about the age of six there was a missionary who used to visit—I think now it was my eldest sister who he

[xxvi]

really did come to visit—he used to tell mother that I looked like I had all the cares of the world on my shoulders. I did not like him a bit for I really did not know what he meant at the time, but he must had had a good look at the future for his words came pretty well true, not the world but quite a good deal of cares. . . .'

Here the fragment ends abruptly. It is undated but all the evidence points to it having been written in 1945 when Jimmy decided to leave for London and Cornwall. The strains and stresses of family life in Glasgow, combined with his rapid disillusionment with the English course at Glasgow University, had obviously proved too much for him. (Apart from the English course proving too conservative and narrowly academic for his interests, he told me later that another small but additional reason for abandoning it was that he had sat a terminal examination, done very well in it, but had later been disqualified when it was discovered he had taken one intended not for first-year students but for advanced ones.) He had also caused his parents, and especially his mother, considerable anxiety by lying in bed very late during the day and wandering the streets at night. And he had also one brush with the police. They said he had spat at them and caused a breach of the peace. He said that he had been wandering around minding no one's business but his own when they had picked him up as a suspicious character and had dragged him to the police station in a far from gentle fashion. But whatever the exact circumstances, it was exactly the kind of situation to rouse him to a pitch of helpless fury. In fact one of the few consolations he could have had at this time was seeing his first critical articles in print. He published at least two in the Glasgow University Magazine, one on 'Surrealism Realised' and another primarily on Ezra Pound, though showing also his appreciation of Auden, Eliot, MacDiarmid, Cummings, and Graham. The latter is introduced by Ezra Pound's lines:

Go my songs, to the lonely and the unsatisfied,
Go also to the nerve-racked, and to the enslaved-by-convention,
Bear to them my contempt for their oppressors,
Go as a great wave of cool water,
Bear my contempt of oppressors.

He himself recalls this first visit to London in the article,

[xxvii]

'Another Damned Scotsman' which appeared in *The Twentieth Century*, September, 1956:

> I had been seventeen when I was last in Soho and I had been a poet—'the greatest poet in the world', if I remember correctly. But I doubt if I remember anything of that period. It was an explosive mixture of ambitions, expectations, love and rebellion, during which I had no reasonable expectations and could enter into no normal relationship with either a man or an idea, much less a place. Everything else was driven away by the caterwauling insecurity of my belief in myself.

But unfortunately there is very little information about these next two or three years, and how he kept himself alive, especially wandering about Europe—he visited Marburg in the German zone and spent three months in Holland in addition to a year in Paris—except for occasional odd jobs, teaching, interpreting, and translating, is an almost complete mystery. He talked very little about this period of his life, except for hinting at one strong emotional entanglement, though what remained constant was his gratitude first to W. S. Graham—though he says even his help couldn't make the poems he was then writing 'anything other than banal'—and later to Wols. Wols helped him practically by getting him work to eke out what he earned by teaching English and Mathematics, a very precarious livelihood, for example by translating Art Catalogues for the Gallerie Drouin in the Place Vendôme, but was to be much more important as a general influence on him, though more through a kinship of spirit than one directly influencing his work. It is not difficult to see why, for Wols, born in Berlin in 1913 and subsequently a student at the Bauhaus, was himself a refugee, a man without a country who had gone to Paris in 1933, worked primarily as a photographer until he was interned for a time in 1939—only then did he begin to paint in earnest—after which he had lived in desperate poverty in the South of France until he could return to Paris after the war. There was something too which appealed to Jimmy in what one art critic has called his 'spiky abstractions in the tachiste style'. (Years later in London Jimmy was to give a talk at an exhibition of his work, a paper unfortunately lost.) But primarily what brought them together was fellow-feeling; Wols' kindness to this strange young man, and Jimmy's search, then as earlier and later for someone or something to guide him. In fact it is one of the most striking features of Jimmy's formative years that he was continually searching for some kind of teacher, though without in the least sacrificing his independence, having completely failed, through no fault of his family as they conceived their duty and responsibility, to find it at home. The roll-call he himself gives—W. S. Graham, Wols, Hugh MacDiarmid, Professor C. M. Yonge—demonstrates this adequately in itself.

He did, however, make one final attempt to reconcile all the conflicting demands he felt by returning in 1949 to his family, Glasgow, and the University, and there he stayed until 1951, his own account of this period being to say the least inadequate. All he writes, as already quoted, is 'I did not complete my degree course. The death of my mother and the illness of my father forced me to get a job—in Aberdeen as a Marine Scientific Assistant.' And we also have his frivolous remark in *Encounter* that he took up Zoology because he wanted 'to write poems about animals.' But while it is perfectly true that he considered the academic study of Eng. Lit. as one of the chief 'enemies of promise' confronting a creative writer, just as later he was to regard the literary life of London, of reviewing, Soho pubs, literary parties and literary gossip, with equal contempt, it is equally true, though he might remark that he had taken up science as the only way open to him if he was to retain an interest in literature, that his interest in science also was very real and profound. Further, while it was lack of money which ultimately forced him to leave Glasgow without a degree, another very important fact—vital for his intellectual and emotional development—was that his mother did not die naturally, but committed suicide, worn out by a life-long struggle against impossible odds and finally defeated by a combination of circumstances in which her anxiety about Jimmy was only one of many items. As Jimmy's half-sister was to write later:

He [Jimmy] and Myer had a very sad life—so did I. He was fortunate in having his own mother—mine died when I was born. Aunty Bertha [Jimmy's mother] was a very fine woman. She was truly good and though my father was a great burden to her, she loved him. Apparently when my mother died my father nearly went out of his mind. . . . I believe if he had had proper treatment things would have been very different. As

[xxix]

years went by father got worse and this led to endless trouble and made Aunty Bertha's life a misery. She stuck by him and shielded him and nursed him. She often came over to see us but she was always loyal.

Jimmy himself naturally did not often speak about all this. He merely told me that he had come home one day as usual and found that she had hanged herself, and that he had taken down her body. He did not expand beyond the facts, nor did I enquire. But from childhood onwards, as her own words testify, and as several people who knew her confirm, she had always, to use MacDiarmid's phrase, 'emitted a sort of desperate unhappiness.' She also suffered, amongst other ailments, from severe nephritis, and many years later, in 1956, Jimmy was to have his mind at least partly eased when talking to a doctor 'who happened to mention that nephritis set up a system of auto-intoxication which often leads to mental degeneration and, sometimes, to suicide.' But in any case the effect on someone of his character needs no underlining.

In Aberdeen he spent the next four years from 1951 to 1955, and in view of his own terse dismissal of his stay there and of what he describes as 'the demoralisation I suffered on shore' for which 'in the end . . . even the considerable periods spent at sea couldn't compensate', some further information is obviously necessary, especially as he himself did not write about Aberdeen as on several occasions he did in Glasgow. Further, despite his dislike of Aberdeen, and sometimes partly because of it, this was a very productive period. He wrote the bulk of *Still and All* there, got the whole of the raw material for *Living Silver*, and contributed to many periodicals in Britain and abroad. He also had time for an enormous amount of reading. What he really disliked was Aberdeen's public face. The town itself, as many people know who know nothing else about it, is built massively and somewhat oppressively almost entirely of grey granite, a material which has many qualities such as solidity and strength, but one which does not lend itself easily to vitality or elegance, let alone colour or gaiety. Primarily, in fact, it is ideal for building banks and tombs. As for Aberdeen's predominant characteristics, they are mainly middle-class respectability and provincial self-satisfaction, and the University makes surprisingly and disappointingly little impact on the general life, being far too much of a self-contained enclave though this, partly,

[xxx]

is for geographical reasons, the main part of it being in the old town well away from the city centre. Secondly, Aberdeen is for the most part supremely indifferent to the arts, and particularly to poetry: if poetry is considered at all, it is usually in terms of the annual Burns mummery or of comfortably local dialect poets. Thirdly, generally because of the dislike of his landladies and landlords for his bohemian way of life, Jimmy was frequently on the move from one set of lodgings to another. And fourthly, his official job was a junior one and much of it mechanical and boring, presenting little challenge to his true scientific enthusiasms. As Dr John Steele, one of his colleagues and friends at the Marine Laboratory writes, 'He would certainly have got a good degree at Glasgow if he had been able to complete his studies, but in Aberdeen he had the disadvantage of doing routine work which was well below his intellectual ability. This left him with a certain bitterness—and it also left him time to try to define his own level of poetic, as distinct from scientific, assurance. As the former developed he became increasingly unwilling to remain within the pattern of the laboratory and of the literary life he found at the perimeter of the University.' But he was actually very lucky in his colleagues at the laboratory, several of whom, including the head, Dr Lucas and Mr Alasdair McIntyre, had wide literary and other interests, while Dr Steele himself, who knew him better than any of the others, had originally specialised in mathematics at London University, had turned down an opportunity of working on atomic energy though remaining fascinated by the problems and moral dilemmas of such scientists as Dr Oppenheimer, and was also very interested in modern philosophers such as Wittgenstein. As Dr Steele writes, 'His superiors were almost excessively lenient, seeing in Jimmy, perhaps, an expression of the literary ambitions latent in many scientists.' This is putting it mildly. As for his contacts with the University, they were few but I think rewarding, especially with Professor Donald Mackinnon, who then held the chair of Moral Philosophy, and with Dr John Holloway, then lecturing in English. He received a great deal of stimulus and encouragement from them—more perhaps than they realised— at a time when he desperately needed both.

Otherwise he was acutely frustrated as a human being, as a member of society, as a scientist, and apart from the recognition of a minute minority, as a poet. In such a milieu, indeed, he very much gave the impression of a young Rimbaud who had wandered by mistake into a businessmen's convention or a suburban tea party, and what got on his nerves most of all was the complete indifference, if not positive antagonism, he usually met with. This both depressed and infuriated him, and from time to time forced him out of his basic shyness and gentleness either into extravagant and eccentric anti-social behaviour, or deeper and deeper into himself. Of course he made little attempt to conform to convention, or to placate people he disliked. Instead he drank a lot, talked a lot, and read his poems aloud in bars to anyone who would or would not listen, all of which, together with his outré appearance —to which he added for a time a wispy Lenin-type goatee beard— struck the average Aberdonian as extremely odd. But two things in particular worried me about him at this time, apart naturally from the fact that at the Marine Laboratory he was engaged on work which almost completely failed to satisfy him. The first was his increasing interest in philosophy and linguistics and especially in Wittgenstein, a matter of frequent discussion with us. This I felt did not blend easily with his equal enthusiasm for the poetry of W. S. Graham, George Barker, and Dylan Thomas, critical though this was, and above all I thought it tended to make his poetry even more cerebral than it already was. Though almost entirely outside my own immediate range of interests, and while generally in entire agreement with the final proposition of the *Tractatus Philosophicus* (interpreting it to suit my own ends)—'Whereof one cannot speak, thereof one must be silent'—I felt I knew enough, and felt strongly enough, to suggest the *Tractatus* was not perhaps one of the best guides for a poet, quite apart from Wittgenstein's fundamental reconsideration of his position in *Philosophical Investigations*. 'Tell him *things*. He'll stand more astonished. . .'. I would quote to him from Rilke, and invite him to analyse Wittgenstein's famous penultimate proposition, No. 6.54, in the *Tractatus*: 'My propositions are elucidatory in this way: he who understands me finally recognises them as senseless, when he has climbed out through them, on them, over them. (He must so to speak throw away the ladder, after he has climbed up on it.)' This was a ladder, it seemed to me, he might well throw away, and after he had got off. And at certain times he himself, obviously, was aware of the dangers. During this period, for example, he was also interested in the possibilities of narrative poetry, in part precisely to avoid overintellectualisation. The chief result of this interest was *The Transparent Prisoner*, and incidentally this poem was neither autobiographical, as some critics not unreasonably guessed, nor fictional. It was based on the actual experiences of a British soldier who had returned to Aberdeen University to complete his studies in Honours English after the war. Jimmy and I met him usually in a pub called The Bond and I still remember Jimmy's excitement as he considered the possibilities of using his story as a theme—the returned ex-prisoner even used the work 'transparent' to describe his emaciated hand against the coal face. Jimmy also met the partisan leader, now naturalised, who helped him to escape. (I do not give their names as neither is the kind of person who likes publicity.) In passing I may say also that the 'Jan' of *Living Silver*, though a composite figure and in part autobiographical, was also largely based on another real person, this time a Pole who had also had a tough war, and who went through the training described. He is now in Canada. Jimmy himself very rarely went to sea on trawlers. He went on the research ships, the *Scotia* and the *Explorer*. This in one sense makes his imaginative reconstruction all the more remarkable, though in another I agree with Geoffrey Grigson and other critics of *Living Silver* that the book might have been more successful as straight science and without using the device of 'Jan' at all. Jimmy used it partly to give human interest, and partly to give him the opportunity of subjective reporting, at which indeed he excelled.

The second thing which worried me, and naturally much more than any literary questions, was his increasingly acute depression. He said to me bitterly one day, 'I drink nowadays just to get drunk—and as quickly as possible.' He also talked again of suicide, and these worries came to a head when one day he asked me to be his literary executor 'if anything happens to me', shortly after this disappearing completely and without warning, taking nothing with him, for about a week, enquiries all over Scotland among his friends producing absolutely no information. However, he returned as unexpectedly as he had left, the first I heard of it being a phone call from his landlord very late at night saying simply 'the wanderer has returned and wants to speak to you', the upshot being that Jimmy, who was in very bad shape, told me that he had decided to go into the local mental hospital as a voluntary patient but refused to do so until he had the personal assurance of the head

[xxxiii]

of mental health, whom he knew to be a friend of mine, that he would not be given electric shock treatment. I did not think for a moment that this could possibly happen without his permission, but Jimmy was adamant, and after a whole day of negotiations, and of telephoning backwards and forwards, it all ended up in my house with a doctor, a psychiatrist, an ambulance team, and his landlord with a taxi. What, however, had initially promised to be a tragedy turned in the end to comedy. In the first place Jimmy refused point blank to go in the ambulance, insisting on the taxi, and also inviting everyone present for a farewell drink at a nearby hotel. And in the second place he telephoned me only three days later to say he was discharging himself because, he said, he could not stand the food. The simple truth is that he had gone away feeling at the end of his tether to try to work things out, and had drunk a great deal, so that when he had a couple of days' rest and the most immediate symptoms had disappeared, he came to the conclusion that the true underlying causes could be cured only by himself and by radically changing his whole way of life.

It was then that he really decided that he must leave Aberdeen, though the actual occasion some time later was a trifling breach of official regulations, the culmination of a series of lapses which his colleagues at the laboratory had most sympathetically overlooked. Indeed they had tried to get him promotion and more interesting work to do. As Dr Steele writes,

> His relations with the laboratory progressed through a series of conflicts which were, partly, a product of his own stresses. After a very successful interview for promotion to a higher scientific post, he extended his discussions with literary friends so long that he arrived back in Scotland just in time to miss a research ship he was supposed to have joined. This cancelled out his achievement in the interview and he remained in the laboratory as a technician. There followed an accumulation of minor misdemeanours. After lunch-time talking and drinking sessions, he preferred cowboy films to the boredom of routine at a bench. These incidents were probably designed to persuade his superiors—and himself—that he should take the plunge into metropolitan literary life to find if he could survive there. The final incident occurred just after the laboratory had received some inadvertent and unfortunate publicity and the ad-

ministration in Edinburgh declared that all contacts with the press must have their approval. Shortly after this the local paper discovered one evening that a centre page article for the next day had not arrived. Between ten p.m. and midnight Jimmy was able to produce a substitute on the work of the Marine Laboratory, its past achievements and its future prospects. The fact that it was a very good article did not save him. . . . Some time later he went through the polite fiction of resigning for reasons of health.

There had also been misdemeanours away from Aberdeen. Once in the Faroes, for example, wandering around alone very late at night, he had seen a single lighted window and had tried to get in through it, cutting his hands badly in the process. The interesting thing, however, is that when his superiors went round next day to apologise and make good the damage, the occupants of the house were far more concerned about Jimmy, whom they had taken in and given first aid, as they had never before, they said, seen anyone who seemed so lost and lonely. Perhaps it is not too fanciful to suggest he may have recalled this incident when later with Jerzy Peterkiewicz he translated a Polish poem by Kasprowicz, certainly one he particularly liked, and of which one verse reads

One evening I got very drunk
—Wine's a good cure, you know.
I punched a window out and gazed
At mountains far away.
There, they said, the snows are lying
And stars that glitter like snow.
Damp darkness fell on my eyelids
And all I saw looked grey.
What matters is dancing.

Only Jimmy, significantly, punched a window in.

His decision to leave was not taken before time. Apart from his disturbed mental state and immediate and local pressures, including some highly complicated emotional relationships with girls, he was receiving pathetic and mystified letters from his father in Glasgow: 'My Dear Jim,' he would write in one, 'I received your most welcome letter, but I am afraid I am unable to understand many parts of it . . . .' Or again, 'Things are much the

[xxxv]

same. I have the opportunity of a good job with *Big Money* but the doctors will not give me the O.K., however I shall try it without them, as things are bad . . .'. Or again, 'Regarding myself things could not be much worse. I took digs at 30/- per week. I get 26/- from the insurance. I cannot go to work yet because the Doctor has not and will not sign me off . . . I am giving up my room to-morrow and shall stay at a nightly hostel . . . in other words I am dead broke, and if you can rush me a few pounds I could use it. . . .' His father was also very anxious that he should make things up with Myer, from whom he had been estranged for some time, and several times insisted that Myer had been very kind and had helped him as much as he could. Meanwhile at the same time his poetry was appearing more and more regularly in periodicals, he had been doing some successful broadcasting, and he had been receiving considerable encouragement from editors, notably that of *The Listener*, who gave him a great boost by printing 'The Transparent Prisoner' in its entirety—the longest poem, I believe, it had ever published—from the various editors of *Lines Review*, from Alexander Scott of *The Saltire Review*, and from Princess Marguerite Caetani of *Botteghe Oscure*. (Indeed one day he might receive a despairing appeal from his father, and on another a telegram from her saying 'Delighted. Magnificent poem. Writing.') It was she too who suggested he should approach Alan Pryce Jones (then editing the *T.L.S.*, for which later he was to write a great deal), who helped him most generously financially as she did so many other talented writers, and incidentally it was in a letter to her from Aberdeen that he explained why he wrote under the name of Burns Singer, a letter which also casts an interesting light on his feelings for his parents:

You were quite right in conjecturing that Burns is my mother's name. My own first name is James, usually pronounced Jimmy. The reasons for the assumption of my mother's surname was that I found that most of my publications—no matter whether they were signed Jimmy, James, or J. H.—were being confused with those of John Singer, for whose lyrical poetry I have a great respect but with whom I don't want to be associated in the public imagination. John himself was no more pleased than I with the consequent uncertainty in the mind of the reading public and even in that of certain editors. . . . Since, therefore, he was the elder I conceded the J. S. formula to him and since, at the time, I was engaged on my Lorca tragedy I decided to adopt the Spanish convention of naming a person after both parents, and thus resolve the ambiguity. It is a step I have never regretted and, especially since my mother's death, I have found satisfaction in reconciling, in my own name, two persons and two families which were never otherwise reconciled— not even, as you might otherwise imagine, in my own life.

The fullest account of his state of mind before going to London, however, is in a letter written while at sea and partly dealing with a suggestion which had been made to him that he might find it useful to have a literary agent, in itself another encouraging gesture. It is headed 'Aboard *F.R.S. Explorer*, North Sea, 7th July, 1955' and I quote extracts:

> I have been going through a rather bad period . . . and even now I am still circumambulating a nervous breakdown, but decisions have been reached and I am in a position to make a few plans.
> First then, let me say that I shall be in London over part of September and it may well be that I shall have to remain there permanently. At any rate I am resigning my present position at the end of this sea-trip which means that I shall be free at the end of August. Should I be forced to take literature as a wife as well as a mistress I will try to avail myself of your kind offers in finding myself a literary agent. Are these still open? Or are you annoyed with my long silence? You shouldn't be. I have posted hardly a letter this year. I have been quite unable to write . . . [however] one of the main reasons for quitting science is that I want to write more and one of the things I want to write is an immense poem about Israel and The Golden Calf. At the moment I am writing from the middle of no-where—which is incidentally a very misty and uncomfortable spot. It will be some days before I reach anywhere and, therefore, before I can post this.

He then discusses various reactions to 'The Transparent Prisoner' and ends as follows:

> Knowing that I am shortly going out into the cold world where I shall probably starve to death (you have no idea how feckless,

improvident, and at the same time, shy, I habitually am) I have taken care to acquire a few things that I would not otherwise have been able to afford. If you can see the logic of these remarks you will see more than I can.

However I have now been home for some time—and I've still not posted this. The nervous breakdown is being kept off—about a nerve's thickness away. The summer is going on and my chest gives me hell.

About his period in London, later in Cambridge, and finally in Plymouth I am not really qualified to speak at first hand. We kept in touch by occasional letters, the late-night phone calls he indulged in, and once he visited Aberdeen, commissioned to write a series of articles for *The Observer* on some of the strange religious sects which flourish in the North East of Scotland—sects such as the Close Brethren—and once I stayed with him in London. The pattern, however, especially in London, is clear and has three fairly distinct if obviously overlapping aspects. The first of these concerns his personal life. London obviously—though his literary prospects were much brighter there than in Aberdeen, a point to which I shall return—was not the place to solve his deep-seated mental problems overnight. In fact in some way it exacerbated them, for here he had to face as a very little-known writer a much more challenging and competitive environment, if a more tolerant one so far as individual eccentricities were concerned, than any he had known before. Further, London's notorious tolerance or 'permissiveness' is often merely indifference, and that was one thing above all which Jimmy could not bear. So in social gatherings he behaved arrogantly and extravagantly, partly perhaps to draw attention to himself, but far more to cover up his basic insecurity. G. S. Fraser in 'Burns Singer: Memories of a Friendship' in *Lines Review*, No 21, Summer 1965, has described this side of him—unfortunately the only side some people saw—very well:

> In London, in fact, he often struck me as being gratuitously rude to poets or reviewers who didn't satisfy his fierce standards of integrity. I have seen him rush away from a literary party at *The Twentieth Century* like a man released from prison, and I have seen him, at the poetry readings which I used to hold at my flat in Chelsea, reduce a very handsome and for all I know talented American Rhodes scholar to tears. Jimmy's father

had been a salesman, rather, so far as I can make out, like the hero of *Death of a Salesman*. Jimmy had a slightly salesman-like attitude to his own wares—'I have just written a g-r-e-a-t po-em', he would say—and a kind of instinctive principle of attack upon the pretensions of possible rivals. He would quite often ask me to read one of my poems aloud and stop me after a line or two with: 'Oh, no, George, it's no good, it's no good!' I didn't mind this, because after all, like all poets who have been working on the craft long enough, I have a certain protective self-conceit; if the impulse has been true, and you have done enough work on the thing, you don't care a damn what anybody says. . . . But I did once get in a fury with him when, in the middle of a large party I was giving, and in ear-shot of everybody, he said: 'Poor George, it's a great pity you can't write decent English prose!' Prose reviewing, broad-casting, translating, was, after all, my bread and butter and kept a roof over my head. I buffeted Jimmy about the head and several of my henchmen, who detested him, were ready to hurl him downstairs. But I almost immediately relented. . . .

Jimmy in London in fact, was a social fire-cracker. As I say, his mind was too serious and committed for that world of parties and literary chatter, in which I felt perfectly at home. When . . . he settled in Cambridge, he came into close and intimate contact with minds he could respect, those of men like John Wisdom, Joseph Needham, Donald Mackinnon, and so far as I can make out he was completely at ease at Cambridge, where in London he was often in a fury, and often a rousing fury.

Later, after describing how Jimmy 'very effectively disrupted a rather important dinner party we were giving for a British Council couple, off to do cultural work in Japan', and remarking that in London 'he blurted out whatever was in his mind and heart, and made enemies everywhere', G. S. Fraser concludes by admitting that he was often 'a source of profound social embarass-ment to me.'

If Jimmy could smash up what I had intended to be a genially superficial social evening, he would; and perhaps, indeed, I often felt in my deep heart that he was right. Perhaps the happiest times I remember with him are the afternoons when, in Chelsea, we would club together for a couple of bottles of cheap Spanish wine and go along to the flat of John Davenport, in Rossetti Mansions. John, the most widely and deeply read man I know, has chosen to talk out (rather than talk away) his genius rather than write it out. I would sit back and listen, largely, while John and Jimmy aired the extraordinary range of their minds. Jimmy was at heart a severe person: Stoic, neo-Calvinist, a believer in harsh self-mastery and the cultivation of a dominating will. He was nevertheless most enchanting when most relaxed and—not most tolerant, for he could never be tolerant—but most forgiving.

One wonders, in passing, just what he had to forgive; the boot, one might think, was very much on the other foot. But these excerpts are not to be seen in isolation. They describe, and accurately, only one side of Jimmy's character, and elsewhere G. S. Fraser pays generous tribute to his talent and to the good sides of him which showed when he was not engaged in outraging people he often thought were posturing dilettantes. One cannot, however, blink the fact that he did behave this way, and that he did make enemies— though in my own opinion those who attend 'regular poetry readings' deserve all they get. In fact I have seen him behave in this manner even when with writers he otherwise respected, and years before I read G. S. Fraser's account I came across a passage in The Captive Mind by Czeslaw Milosz which seemed to fit him very well:

Behind his words one felt a mixture of arrogance and humility. In conversation he seemed inwardly convinced of his own superiority; he attacked ferociously. . . . His ripostes were full of pent-up irony. Probably, though, these characteristics were most pronounced when he spoke with other writers older than he. As a beginning poet, he felt he owed them a certain respect, but actually he believed they were none too deserving of it. He knew better; in him lay the promise of a truly great writer.

But I soon recognised this for what it was, a desperate front put on to mask the conflict between his driving ambition and inner uncertainties. I also knew his background.

Despite such behaviour in public, however, the second and far more important feature, was that, as his output shows, he was

[xl]

doing a great deal of work. He had renewed and strengthened old literary contacts and he had made many new ones. He was contributing poems to many periodicals. He reviewed regularly for the *T.L.S., The Listener, Encounter*, and so on. He broadcast. He scripted the commentary for a documentary film and had plans for others. He also had plans, and in several cases signed contracts, for several books, including one on his home town, Glasgow, and another, which promised to be far more ambitious, a comprehensive study, in four parts, of Scotland past and present, to be called *Created Free*, and he even envisaged a complete history of Scottish literature ('anything from six to a dozen substantial volumes,' he wrote to his publisher), on which at one time he intended to spend intermittently the rest of his life, first learning Gaelic. Consequently—even allowing again for the Coleridgean element in some of his proposals—everything seemed on the surface set fair for him professionally, or as fair as the hazardous business of living by one's pen can ever be. While the third feature, also following soon after his arrival in London, promised best of all—and fulfilled much of that promise—his marriage to Marie Battle, the black American psychologist a year after meeting her at the home of a mutual friend. At first, however, things went far from smoothly. Jimmy was still in private suffering from bouts of acute depression, and on one occasion attempted suicide. Marie, who had completed her training in London, had been invited to go back to the States for a time to lecture at Yale and Smith College, her *alma mater*, while Jimmy went to stay at Cheddar in Somerset where he worked on *Living Silver* and awaited the publication of *Still and All*, both of which were to appear a year later in 1957. The separation was a comparatively short one, like Marie's absence, but even so his letters surviving from the period show a man who has gone through a great deal but who feels that he will—that he *must* pull through. One letter, written in April 1956, shows his state of mind very well at this time, and it is particularly interesting as showing his reaction to such success as he had had:

> I have, during the past three years, had far too easy a sucess. I have not had to try hard enough. The results for a little effort have always been too immediate and too great. Everybody has been too kind to me. This agent just now is being wonderful. Through it all I remember George Barker's warning: 'You just

wait, baby, till they all start sticking knives in your back.' He was reprimanding me for my attempted suicide. And I think too of the words in his new play: 'The morality of despair is: *Keep going. Go on.*' There are some men who can be trusted only in matters of life and death. He is one of them. And he can be trusted absolutely. It was he, as well as you, who kept me alive, his poetry and his person. But the suicide danger has passed.

And 'From now on I shall write . . .' becomes a continual cri-de-coeur. Yet he realises he is very tired, physically and mentally. 'I must have been very undernourished when I met you,' he writes to Marie in one letter—he is suffering from boils—and in another, 'I'm beginning to think that I was vastly overworked in Aberdeen. Then, when I came to London, I began to rest, and the real nervous exhaustion became visible. . . .' And again he writes 'I am beginning to be able to relax', but in fact he is continually vacillating between lethargy and activity, apathy and ambition:

> Yet the strange thing is that, during all this dilatory dallying, I do not feel at peace with myself—not for one moment. . . . The whole thing shows how far I have fallen off since ten years ago. Then I would have been continually filled with that contented excitement which characterises the man who has something to do. I am beginning to face the fact of my utter aimlessness. For the past four years I have been managing along somehow from the impetus of my adolescence. But now I am coming to a full stop. Can't go on much longer. Something must kick me into motion. You give me a kick, baby. . . My spirit is sick, baby. . . .

And in another letter he says that, 'Today I feel a little like Keats, just arrived in the Isle of Wight. I wish I felt more like him. That was the beginning of his *annus mirabilis*. . . .' He also has the usual doubts about the value of what he is actually producing. 'Pretentious drivel,' he writes at one point after re-reading some work. . . . 'Christ, I wish I could write something decent. Just one thing.' For it is quite clear that he always applied to himself standards quite as high, indeed higher, than he did to others, a subject on which he amplifies after Marie has expressed admiration for a poem he didn't think much of:

> I don't understand your admiration for *Gold*. It's not really a

very good poem, though it is quite interesting as an experiment. A lot of the diction is bloated, and a good deal stilted. The images haven't the kind of direct appeal necessary for a poem. But then I think you far too prone to admiration about everything. Think, there are probably only two or three good English poets alive, certainly not more than six. It could be unlikely for them all to be immediately recognised. Of the people I know only Barker has a chance, and that a slim one. Certainly not dear old ———. One must not be generous in this kind of assessment. To be generous is to encourage the mediocre, and the mediocre is to be abominated. ———'s poetry is mediocre.

And all this applies to painting, and psychoanalysis. Before it is worth trying to do any of these things, one must be so superlatively good at them that there is *literally* not a soul alive who is as good at it. The so-called 'arrogance' of artists is the result of their knowledge of this fact. They continually say that they are the 'best alive' because they know that if they are not there is no possible justification for their existence at all. A poem can't be 'good'. It must be the best—though there is probably a potentially infinite number of best poems. Art works in terms of superlatives. You must understand that. The only *raison d'être* it can possibly establish is the witness of its perfection. For perfection is significance. Nothing else is of any importance. *What* is perfected matters much less than is usually thought, for perfection consists of the delicacy of the balance between the parts rather than in the nature of the parts themselves.

These things are absolutely true. There is no doubt whatever, and every artist knows them to be true. But again, their direct opposites are also true. The greatness of a work of art depends finally on the amount of life that is put into it, the amount of experience it covers, and it doesn't matter a damn if it is imperfectly organised provided you pack enough into it.

You have thus two truths—the 'classical' and the 'romantic' —and they are both true, and they are true all the time. There can be no attempt to reconcile them. Their truth finally consists in their opposition to one another. There is thus no problem, merely a set of emotional and formal facts. To try to transform it to the linguistic level (i.e. to make a problem out of it) is to miss the essence of the experience and to obliterate its significance.

I do not offer this because of its coherence, or because I agree with the opinions where I can indeed reconcile them. (We talked often enough, in all conscience, about such matters—about Joyce's epiphanies, the very useful function performed, so far as I was concerned, by so-called 'minor' poets—and disagreed amicably but firmly and finally.) I offer it rather as his fullest attempt, outwith his published and broadcast criticism, to formulate an aesthetic.

It is not for me to discuss anything so private as Jimmy's life with Marie except to say that clearly she was to give him more happiness than he had ever known before. She also gave him more stability, a centre, and a home, the first he had ever really known, especially when they moved away from the frenetic atmosphere of London and its literary Bohemia to settle in Cambridge. Meanwhile both *Still and All* and *Living Silver* received very good notices, if in the case of the former some rather puzzled ones. The recommendation of *Still and All* by the Poetry Book Society was an additional and very welcome vote of confidence, and one, of course, which guaranteed it wider circulation and more attention that it might otherwise have had as a first book of poems, while the American edition of *Living Silver* was also favourably received. He was busy, too, in his collaboration with Jerzy Peterkiewicz on their translations of Polish poetry, and as always, with whatever birth pangs and self-questionings, prolific with poems, articles, and reviews. His future promised, in fact, to be more settled than ever before, yet he was still dogged by ill-health, worry, and depression. In 1959, for example, before moving to Cambridge, he went to Spain for a holiday, for some sun, and to recuperate, and though several letters from there are cheerful enough—apart from the inevitable financial troubles—one, to Marie, is still acutely pessimistic:

> Still unable to work. The review of Christine's book, three-quarters done, lies on my table in continual reproach. But really I am unable to do anything. I cannot even carry on a conversation. I feel so utterly stupid when talking to an intelligent person, like Josef or Gerald, and so utterly bored when talking to a stupid one. [Josef Herman and Gerald Brenan—both of whom had been very kind to him.] I don't know how

[xliv]

to escape from this pattern of inarticulateness. It spirals up and up, driving ever more complicated wedges between me and the outside world. So I am quite relieved when I can lie alone, like now, and just think—though none of my thoughts is very interesting either. No artificial stimulus does any good. When I get drunk I don't quarrel with anybody, I don't assert myself, I don't write, I don't talk. In all company I am continually nervous. Alone I am even more agitated. What on earth will happen to me I can't imagine. I seem to have lost all will to go on living. And yet I am quite comfortable. I simply don't understand what has happened, but I do know that whatever it is has been happening for a long time. This is no sudden depression but the negative side of my whole life up to the present. I grow giddy at the thought of how far it all goes back and how deeply inwoven into the very stuff I am made of. But 'that passed over, and so may this'—perhaps it will—at any rate I must be patient and wait for it to happen.

'That passed over, and so may this. . . .' It is, of course, an echo of the refrain of the Anglo-Saxon poem *Deor*, the lament of the exiled poet—'thaes ofereode, thisses swa maege.' Also this letter ends on a more hopeful note, with Jimmy looking forward to the idea of living in Cambridge, where he and Marie were to live, in Little St Mary's Lane, for most of the next four years, in much more congenial surroundings, and altogether in happier circumstances. Even there, however, Jimmy felt increasingly the insecurity of earning his living primarily from reviewing, journalism, and occasional broadcasts, and increasingly tired too of the ephemeral nature, as he considered it, of much he consequently had to produce, so as time went past his thoughts turned more and more to returning to marine biology. This was a project which both his literary and scientific friends and acquaintances encouraged, Kathleen Raine, for example, a poet he much admired, sending him some admirably sane advice, while Professor Carl Pantin, Professor of Zoology at Cambridge, arranged for him to spend six weeks in the spring of 1963 at the Marine Laboratory at Plymouth, and was later instrumental in getting him a Leverhulme Fellowship to return there to carry out a research project in June 1964. *Living Silver* was already known and appreciated there by members of the Council. Nor is there any doubt of the enthusiasm with which he returned to original work—on the problem of *Ampelisca* speciation—nor that he had the skill to carry it out, as Dr Eric D. S. Corner, one of his colleagues there to whom I am deeply indebted for information about this last period of his life, fully confirms. Old habits, however, cannot be cast off overnight, and after paying tribute to his ability and the difficulty of the task he had set himself, Dr Corner writes, not unexpectedly, as follows:

> The problem that Jimmy had chosen to investigate and his method of doing so demanded considerable skill and application . . . but other things distracted him. He maintained his literary activities—notably book reviewing—all the time he was here, and became keenly interested in the possibility of preparing material for television—a documentary about trawlers. He had earlier provided a commentary to a film called *Between the Tides*, and this was highly regarded by various people in the profession. . . Apart from these interests he made several journeys to see other writers in the South East, including Colin Wilson and Charles Causely and—you will not be surprised to learn—he also spent a good deal of time in various pubs, entertaining numerous people with his views on literature, especially poetry. He was a great reader and a great drinker and these sessions often lasted late into the afternoon, and often late at night as well. They were excellent value . . . but they were hardly consistent with the need to tackle a demanding research programme. Yet Jimmy was genuinely enthusiastic about research—and often claimed that the scientist and the poet had much in common, as each was exclusively concerned with the search for truth. Certainly *Living Silver* seems to me to reveal a wonderful gift for making an immensely readable account of a very complicated subject without oversimplifying to the point of inaccuracy, though Jimmy himself once told me that it was really an early example of the anti-novel. . . .

Jimmy would. That remark is entirely typical of his deprecatory and sardonic humour, an aspect of his character to which I have perhaps paid too little attention, not because I didn't appreciate it—I did so profoundly—but because it does not lend itself at all easily to reproduction. Like almost everything about him it was uniquely personal.

He died suddenly, in Plymouth, four months after going there, on the night of the 8th September 1964. There were rumours of suicide. Dr Corner mentions them locally, and they also very quickly reached Scotland. It is therefore necessary to state categorically that his death was due to natural causes, to *a*. Myocardial Lichaemia, and *b*. Atheromatous coronary occlusion. (I quote from his death certificate.) There was a post mortem, but no inquest. He was cremated and the ashes were scattered at sea from a research trawler, the *Sarsia*. And two years later, on 24th July 1966, a memorial stone was dedicated to his memory in Little St Mary's Churchyard, Cambridge. But his best epitaph, it is perhaps superfluous to say, are his poems. Many of them are concerned with death. Several of them are concerned with his own death—for example, *Requiescat*, *Preparation*, and perhaps most apt of all, *Epilogue:*

That death might not be casual,
Flick thumbing ash in the swish of a squint draught,
Lint pad for a bruise-eyed nation,
Bandage to blindfold memories that laughed;
That death might not be an empty flesh-felt gesture:

That hereafter might not be fed
With mutes mad and the sane ones poor and scared,
An asylum from single beds,
From the profane ignorance everywhere shared;
That God might not be a charitable institution for the dead:

I wrote these verses down
And left them and was gone.

For this book 'Collected' does not mean 'Complete'. I have excluded juvenilia, a considerable number of occasional poems, unfinished poems, etc. Burns Singer was a very prolific poet. He wrote enormously and prodigiously, anywhere, at any time, and on anything—odd scraps of paper, the backs of envelopes, even on the dustjackets of books. Further, some of his poems are untitled, others exist in different drafts, and many are undated. Apart from those he himself chose for *Still And All*, the collection published in 1957, arrangement has presented peculiar difficulties.

W. A. S. Keir

[xlvii]

STILL AND ALL

Still and All

I give my word on it. There is no way
Other than this. There is no other way
Of speaking. I am my name. I find my place
Empty without a word, and my word is
Given again. It is nothing less than all
Given away again, and all still truly
Returned on a belief. Believe me now.
There is no other. There is no other way.

These words run vertical in their slim green tunnels
Without any turning away. They turn into
The first flower and speak from a silent bell.
But underneath it is as always still
Truly awakening, slowly and slowly turning
About a shadow scribbled down by sunlight
And turning about my name. I am in my
Survival's hands. I am my shadow's theme.

My shadow's ground feeds me with roots, and
    rhymes
My statement over. Its radius feeds my flames
Into a cool tunnel. And I who find your ways
About me. (In every part I find your ways
Of speech.) pierce ground and shadow still. The light
Is struck. Its definition makes me my quiet
Survival's answer. All still and all so truly
Wakening underneath me and turning slowly.

It's all so truly still. I'll take you into
The first statement. I'll take you along cool tunnels
That channelled light and petalled an iridescent
Symmetry over my bruised shadow. And yes
I'll take you, and your word will follow me,
Till definitions gather distilled honey
And make their mark the fingerprints of light.
I am, believe me then, the name I write.

I lie here still. Yes, truly still. And all
My deliberate identities have fallen
Away with the word given. I find my place
In every place, in every part of speech,
And lie there still. I let my statements go.
A cool green tunnel has stepped in the light of my
    shadow
There is no way round it. It leads to the flower
Bell—that swings slowly and slowly over.

18IIIXSG

  This is for afterwards.
I've heard it calling halfway what I mean
By my own name. I've heard it out and made
My answer alter all the words between
Us as we spoke them up through the unsaid.
What was all mine, all none of us, is ours.
I move away from what I must endure
Afterwards. Its meaning green and upward stares
But blank across the meaning plods a boor.
This is the end of me. It's always been
This way from what I am. I'm renegade
To what I am. Between us language roars
Its floods to drown me in. My death is sure:
Though safe to watch me going down we stand
Beside ourselves with horror on dry land.

  All that then afterwards.

Meanwhile my mouth goes on to promising
That this gay night is half the night it was
When, without voice, half of the moon could sing
Through Marazion to each one of us.
I've half undone it, hearing what I make
Almost it say to me. I'm there again
And, being there, the words forget to take
Immediately to the wound that feels the pain.
And yet it hurts. You know it hurts, but fling
That speaking through us each aside for laws
Where everything is measured up to fake
And tiny thunders or some coloured rain
Grow big enough to drown. A full moon sways
Over the piece of us that each betrays.

[5]

Hear then now afterwards.

I'll talk against the way I'm talking to
This devil at my elbow with his pins
Through my parsed mind. He makes it try to do,
Impossibly through spreadeagled synonyms,
For things that almost happened but could not.
It's half my way with you to be half lost.
It's all of it I pack in the least thought.
And when I've done we do not know the most.
We're all behind before we've started through
The syllables, but the syllable as it spins
Loud out long after us, it's not not not
Nothing nor next to it, nor best, nor worst,
But always halfway what we say to each
Till, having spoken, we discover speech.

Your Words, My Answers

Then what is it I am
To make of what I mean?
What words will take it down
Through the disputed realm
Where you and I across
An oblique imperative
Meet one another's loss?
Let that fierce statute give
Us new authority
Which takes away our claim
To saying what we mean:
Like the two limbs of a cross
Your words, my answers lie
Together in the place
Where all our meanings die.

The Love of Orpheus

See, he is stooping. A thousand flavours rise
In the sun, melt away in his singing mouth,
Yet he bends down hard as potato-pickers for wages,
This slim stark god antiquity makes gorgeous;
And supple as sand in the sweet sway of his youth
He follows his woman through final immensities.

Among brown roots, brown hair of the new to die,
Roots of some streets as well as trees, like lice
He crawls an intruder, bold and alive; he clinks
In his clothes, heavy at heels with coins, trinkets,
Tokens, embarrassed to anger by luck of their noise
As he falls like an army on final immensities.

Then the long passage of colliding souls,
The deeper dead who meet in the dark to growl,
Gossip and kiss: he crowds among them too. No.
They frighten him. He stops. They almost grow
Weapons and limbs, lamp-posts gone on the prowl,
But are motionless, pitiful, thin there and savagely
    cold.

Or, if he moves at all, like water bread
Goes pale and salt, comes back and eddies forth
Through tumbling ghosts of worried men—among
Them sinking slow: through songs that are scraping
    his tongue,
With his breath clotted as bones, wild faith in her
    worth,
Wild grief in her death, Orpheus sways tormented.

Times to go back to labours innocent
As seedlings, birds at song in the sunlight pecking,
Layers of daybreak building up a square
To the great traffic trundling everywhere,
Times to go back creep up at each step taken.
Yet he, for her fair-headed sake, descends

Always again towards the final immensities,
No, not for her. Rather for any, all
Comfort or cubicle, shelter from ghosts with their
    guilt:
A conscript boy, called-up from his mother's milk
To be suckled till death to murder, knows as well
The man he shoots as Orpheus what he seeks.

That he discovers later. Imagine now
And now, and now, and now, the trials he takes
Backwards and forwards, nearer, then the river
Wrapped in its delicate climate, seeing him, shivers.
His young face trembles in the wrinkled wake
Of Charon's steerage, going slow and slow.

And frogs, and frogs, the chatter and clatter of frogs,
Creaking and croaking—a musty mahogany flamework,
Victorian sideboards crashing to ashes and more
Sinking the roof to the floor, gurgle and roar;
—A house falls in on his head, braining the frame-
    work,
Or, heavily, steadily, water, dropping by drops.

Quite suddenly it stops. He stands bewildered.
As if an army at the pitch of battle
Simply forgot to fight, stood still to wonder
Fearlessly at the dead, he turns almost as tender.

Shades are whining like women, shawls on their
    brittle
Bodies, shuffling like gravel, like biscuits, like child-
    hood,

Loud and embarrassing underneath his ears,
Noisy and old and cold as all of us.
And these were the cute ones, swift with enchantment,
    press
Of life's wine, the white and the red of the blood. These
Were his mistresses, gentle ones, hard ones to please.
They lie like linen that can't dry for showers

Or stiff as soldiers ice has cooled, but dead,
Always, as dolls. O, is it love then or shame
That drives him like snow towards the final immen-
    sities?
His least step now, these last perplexities
Will finish, be folded away, revealing the doomed
House, pillar on plain black pillar, black instead.

Even then the bricks can sparkle, sharp and tiny,
Intense or less intense. It is as though
A scaffolding of cobwebs, mite by mite,
Holds busy masons who surpass the night
In spidering silence, erect a climbing glow
That sparks where darkness hits it, black and shiny.

Sheen of the dark-edged stones, shine that reflects,
Mirror by river, the lips of the dead, the palace
Black as bee's stripes, to Orpheus hidden in prayer.
He cannot quite remember who or where,
Why, what or how he is, he comes, but always
His journey, that's heavy and hard to bear, connects,

Makes sense: for the first time only he knows he is
    there.
There are quiet attendants to greet with a sleek
    smile
This thumbnail digger who tunnelled away on his
    own:
The passages grow wide to hasten him in,
And a king waits silent, eyes, hands, legs, all still,
In a storm of stillness, dead steady, like animals
    stare.

'Because she loved me, because he is dead, I have
    come.'
From all that's question, somewhat like a diver
Dipping for pearls by Capricorn or Cancer,
He chose just that one sentence for an answer,
Chose it as swarthy hunters choose to deliver
Their bodies to hazard the sea, one place in the
    foam.

And the natural glance of an oyster's cargo and trove
Was laid ajar by his jump, his hurried answer.
She rose in her perfumed image, ikon glow,
Delicious and severe, to undergo
The praise and faith that fell from him like dancers,
High-fevered dancers, leaves, the fall of love.

'For otherwise than women's lovelight glistens
She had an eye—the marrow of a sunbeam—
That even under eyelid harnessed rainbows,
And her long lashes were like pointed rain.
Her tugging pulse, together tender skin
Lay fine as fur, the channels of her wrist.

'Quick as a lemon the taste of her tongue; her teeth
Were gentle as milk. Sweets of her blood—they
    swayed
A tree of smiles, delved rivers in her face,
Cupped hands like petals filled and fresh with grace,
And voices I had lost one voice were made,
A multitude with banners and a faith.

'O why enumerate the special parts?
She was good land, fragrant, where fertile skies
Let fall their various wonders, sun and rain:
With red abandon like a poppy when
She curled up close about me, breast and thighs:
Now gold abundance on the thresher's cart.'

And for that second through eternity
The dead are easy. Tantalus' scorched lips
Suck comfort in. The sisters of the well
Sit on their steps and laugh to be in Hell.
The love of Orpheus like an ointment drips
On the sores of the ghosts throughout final immen-
    sities.

Hush at a far-fetched zenith, climb as soft
As the tumultuous treading upwards, on,
Of busy sunlight through the freckled earth.
Then, very humanly, shuffling backwards and forth
On bony arguments to hold his own,
He tricks to persuade through many elaborate shifts.

'The naked treachery of every vice
Has sweated through my skin. This small white
    body,
These blue eyes, are nowhere ignorant.

[12]

Hell would itself seem almost arrogant
To boast such pensioners, to hold such bloody
And obscene delights, such pettiness.

Cheat, and a liar, and irresolute
Even in evil, a traitor and a coward,
Stupid, incapable, tantalised by thoughts
Too big and honest, loyal to deceit
Down to the hem I kiss that death's embroidered:
From head to foot a queer and shallow brute.

'Yet I near her am cleansed, like molten ore
Into her body's metal am there cast
To an alloy that's precious and powerful, moulded
   and proof.
I, who am most unworthy of her love,
Am by that love made worthy of the rest,
Am onewhere raised, one way brought near, held
   home.

'In the belled silk of her body, bobbin and round
Cocoon, I am made precious a maker as works
With fibres and gums in the green of the mul-
   berry's leaves;
And because there is one who lives left believes
In the strength of his purpose the sun comes up
   like a bird,
Goes gay right through the good and evil earth.

'And men are in our lives worthy, and gentle as
   olives,
And money grows fruitful and free, its paper is pulp,
And the healing faith I instil, that I have in them,
Is given and taken without caution or shame.

[13]

I beg. I beg—not only for her help—
To construct a new kind of riches where death is
    absolved.

'Think of the thick of it, brim to the bottom of luck,
For your black sheriffs a battle, final allegiance
Of millions transmuted to what our minute fulfils.
See how they congregate. The weight that all
Their holiness brings tribute to your patience
Must change your jealousy to miracle.

'Otherwise there is nothing I can do
With the sullen shapes of a sun I cannot distinguish.
I'd better come to an end to plead like a pauper
For a place by her feet whose fate cannot be altered.
Then maybe somebody will, in the toss of anguish,
Remember Orpheus was once denied by you

'And be afraid to follow after him.'
But Pluto smiled and mumbled mistily:
'You talk of faith. Well, have some faith in me
And you will have her back. Now, let me see.
Go on ahead. She'll follow bye-and-bye.
No, not just that. This isn't quite a whim.

'Think deep in love and you will understand.
All that the sun does not see, that is mine:
If you look back what follows is your hope
And, should you see it, is within my grip.
She, who once was, will wait you in the sun.
Think deep in love. This has not been determined.'

[14]

The ghosts now are gone in their magical wardrobes'
      most peaceful
Parade of their habits to sleep, sleep deep as he
      passes.
They are so still and white it is as though
Loud swooping waters stiffened at a blow
And, in a tempest's uproar, salt white horses
Stopped dead in their mid-prance and listened for
      only a breeze.

Or is it nearer like a little child
Who, having howled and huffed the evening out,
Is the poor rascal midnight finds asleep
Upon his pillow far too tired to sleep?
As Orpheus leads upwards like a shout
And his wife follows, quiet, of their kind.

Like a Yankee Clipper over a summer sea
In his silver journeys, beside her, the great god moves
Who whistles winds that whine but come to heel.
Only there are no colours, no silver or steel,
But only a blur that they swerve into like leaves
Stripped for a race and racing from the tree.

A blankness numb as a star, and, like a star
In stillness, is not still through lack of motion
But because of the unmoving distance
Cannot move, or seem to move, is pasted
Millions of years of light away in rotation
That's faster than ours, is held there, still as a star.

And through this quietness three quiet bodies
Move with one footstep nobody can hear.
A spangled hall, the circus silence when

[15]

Three acrobats are up, one rope begins
To stagger underneath them and you hear
The audience grow silent with applause

Would, in this context, seem a fireside chat.
For, as each step grows longer by a heartbeat,
A hair's breadth further back goes Orpheus' thought,
Till like long hair a gale has straightened out
His sense of sound is struggling flimsily backwards
Searching some definite sign, some final support.

But there is nothing. Silence is everywhere.
Not even a cough to excuse it, not even a fight,
Jabber of gossip feuds to reassure him
That maybe their footsteps are lost, that voices ob-
    scure them.
If she were there she'd call, she'd cry, and yet . . .
Long tongues of doubt, milk-mad, or jabbed with
    fire,

Thousands a moment, press, impress his mind.
If by a miracle of mere mistake
Its answer should be wrong, there is no man
Who, with the dead about him, will again
Achieve such strength to choose or, choosing, take
So great a risk of being twice condemned.

First he is sure that somewhere there behind
She is alive and coming after him.
Soon in the sunlight—will it be by nightfall?—
They in twin terror fastened for a while
Will walk the various world, have children and fame,
All the round riches gather ever designed.

But, as the silence has it otherwise,
He will alone learn how the gods can cheat,
Their mercies worse than man's mere cruelty.
His life will be lived with shy ghosts who defy
Death by inanity, whose closed lives defeat
Each motion in him from his loneliness.

And yet . . . O maybe like a sound too high
For human ears to catch it, she is there
In fact of beauty. To turn then would undo,
Would murder now, would do death brutally
On all that's lovely in a woman's hair,
That loosening sunlight from a bunch of sky.

But away there already another sunlight, a circle,
Draws the conclusion tighter. There it is.
Who, at the sight of this goat, of this mock giraffe,
Pledged to preserve his neck that's only a laugh
And anyhow that isn't even his,
Won't giggle when they see the poor fool tumble?

Yet he, at one turn of a ready head,
Could give the bad lie into good hands forever,
Unslave his sloven race from the false promise
That stiffens and darkens the final immensities.
There would be no excuse, there could be never
A man who toadied, traded his life with the dead.

Nevertheless as timorously as
The first of life, mosaic bred from some
Mud or slow crystal, learned to multiply,
Take nourishment from nitrates, stock the sky
In its arrangement of the carbon atoms,
And so to change the firmament that was.

Immense and dead about it, planets, suns,
With not a thing among them precedent
To this small newness, timorously he,
Half-hoping to turn back, turned round to see
—No, not her beauty's lasting last command—
But mildewed lineaments and worm-worked skin.

And we will never know what would have been
Better or worse, except that here and there
A still-unworshipped god confirms his state
With simple trials or tremendous hate
Or prayers so terrible that none dare hear
Lest all their lives should never then atone.

A Letter

Tonight I'll meet you: yes, tonight. I know
There are, perhaps, a thousand miles—but not
Tonight. Tonight I go inside. I take
All the walls down, the bric-a-brac, the trash,
The tawdry pungent dust these months have
    gathered
Into a heap about me. I must prepare
And somehow move away from the slow world,
The circling menace with its throat and teeth
Attempting definition; and brush off
Those thoughts that, clinging like thin fallen hairs,
Make me unclean: for I must go tonight
And, secret from my shadow, go alone
Back to the hour when you yourself became
So much my own that even my own eyes
Seemed strange compared to you who were a new
Complete pervasive organ of all sense
Through which I saw and heard and more than
    touched
The very dignity of experience.

Verses from a Distance

Gently, my darling, I will hurt by saying
But the one word that it would hurt to silence.
I smother it in every syntax, miming
With different motions but a constant meaning
Till strangers marvel at my way of living.

They see a hurry that is hardly living;
They hear me babble yet I am not saying
Any word, am simply breaking silence,
Silence that seeps out through my heart's miming,
My heart that's breaking with its sense of meaning.

A sense significant but hardly meaning,
More than the wind because it moves is living,
Or than the sea because it sounds is saying,
For my whole heart is breaking into silence
And its disruption is a kind of miming.

Concordant movement that is hardly miming
Of pieces that were blasted with their meaning
Into a new and anxious way of living
Becomes the content of what I am saying
In a vocabulary made of silence.

Soundless intelligence that is hardly silence
Goes out from me through this disordered miming,
Out to my darling who will know the meaning
Of the calamity that we are living
Who cannot speak what our two lives are saying.

A hope, a prayer perhaps, but hardly saying,
Since the whole syntax of our love is silence
And all love's motions are in us made miming:
Maimed and unable is our love's true meaning:
Only the sorrow in us is left living.

Poem

Now absence is a habit it is time
To pack the splendid images away
And send them off in buses that can climb
Up ladders or down snakes as must they may.

For absence is a habit hard to learn
And those who have it haven't much to say.
Their small advice: they live on what they earn
And put the wounded images away.

Tristran and Iseult

Lay them beside each other in the subway.
              Link hands in prayer
              But do not stare.
Such obsequies might strike them as disturbing.

They have no need for death now. That will come
              Like a voice on
              The telephone
When they're shut up in bedrooms, bored and glum.

Yet it will not make any sudden break
              Into their lives
              Where now it thrives
Like mud that thickens in a stagnant lake.

He has forgotten the great god of love
              And the terrific
              Silent traffic
They kept between them as the waters move.

He has forgotten her. In his mind now
              His business debts
              Like silhouettes
With daggers and revolvers steal the show.

Yet it was she who in the sullen attic
              Made him attempt
              To implement
Success which now is talked of as 'dramatic'.

[23]

Words have so many sides when one remembers,
　　　　Looks such large focus:
　　　　His own death's raucous
Croak in his throat seems sweeter than the simpers

Of distant giants, gentle once, he murdered.
　　　　Where they once stood
　　　　Splendid in blood
He finds them dead, or their large bodies shudder

Decrepit, insubstantial, and sparse:
　　　　Laid side by side,
　　　　Hero and bride,
The squalid victims of a royal farce.

If she remembers anything at all
　　　　It's not impassioned
　　　　Cunning legend.
The king, her father's ghost, seems crude and
　　dismal.

His money sweated out of Chinese peasants,
　　　　Irish dockers,
　　　　And street-walkers,
Money he spent in shooting ducks and pheasants;

His bathing pool, a watery Taj-Mahal,
　　　　Surrounded by
　　　　A delicate sky
Which stokers heated in an oven hole;

His porcelain, his catalogued Greek trifles,
　　　　His jewelry's
　　　　Intensities,
The stuffed heads in his library of rifles;

[24]

And all the bands and pageants of
                His followers
                Are not now hers,
Nor is the tingling of her foregone love.

Yet Tristran, he, with her alone, they say,
                Has in a song
                From right and wrong
Taken all malice and the need to pray.

'We have been told' or 'It has been reported'
                There's no appliance
                Of art or science
Can bring us nearer why their love aborted.

Maybe her marriage with its ache of duty,
                Its household shopping,
                Court be-bopping,
Compulsory affection, mirth and beauty,

Varnished the starlight in her, quenched cool water,
                And made her nature
                Imitate her
Till she was posing as her father's daughter.

Or maybe it was him, fond of heroics,
                Who thought that by
                Trying to die
He could enrich love and confound the stoics.

Maybe he thought that by his length of journeys,
                His tricks of valour,
                Apparent squalor,
He made love perfect though he left it mourning.

[25]

But anyhow they travelled out, denying
Love in each other;
And, looking further,
Their backstair past-times seem no cause for dying.

Martyrs at last to what they neither wanted
Though yet we hear,
Year after year,
Their tomb lives echo with the truth they taunted.

Lay them beside each other in the subway.
Death will encroach.
O do not watch.
Their lack of loveliness will set you sobbing.

The Brush-off

You pass politely away
Back among the shrill pygmies.
Their bare faces project
Like clocks about me.

This one has a name.
It hurries up to me.
While that one gives away
All I have wasted.

The clocks are very kind.
Each in its narrow circle
Charmingly reflects
Empty precision.

And each one in return
Asks nothing more of me
Than to represent
A life that's mine.

I watch their flat pale faces
And the black numerals
Till you, my chequered darling,
Disappear inside.

Sunlight

It was a dream in night,
The pier all ropes, a road,
Houses, tiles a-tilting,
Where only sunlight stood.

My bus was made of bridges,
Words I had overheard,
Small streets and talking cages,
Shells that secreted a bird.

It was the South of France.
I climbed the high-built bus
In a sparse but limitless landscape
I knew I could not pass.

So I reversed the corner.
I did not turn. I jumped.
And down on me hard and heavy
Mountains of sunlight were dumped,

With an English pub in the centre
Where wines were cold and dry
And I could feel that sunlight's
Smooth intensity.

Therefore farewell, my lovely;
It was towards you I went
When into dreams at midnight
Summer sunlight bent.

Peterhead in May

Small lights pirouette
Among these brisk little boats.
A beam, cool as a butler,
Steps from the lighthouse.

Wheelroom windows are dark.
Reflections of light quickly
Skip over them tipsily like
A girl in silk.

One knows there is new paint
And somehow an intense
Suggestion of ornament
Comes into mind.

Imagine elephants here.
They'd settle, clumsily sure
Of themselves and of us and of four
Square meals and of water.

Then you will have it. This
Though a grey and quiet place
Finds nothing much amiss.
It keeps its stillness.

There is no wind. A thin
Mist fumbles above it and,
Doing its best to be gone,
Obscures the position.

This place is quiet or,
Better, impersonal. There
Now you have it. No verdict
Is asked for, no answer.

Yet nets will lie all morning,
Limp like stage scenery,
Unused but significant
Of something to come.

Rhapsody

Hello, it's twilight. Put
The clock on top of straight
Against then. And let
Outcry go down as that
'Tick-tock' in goodness what.

And let this twilight bring
A charm to ring-a-ring
Gladness from ghosts among
Absurdities that sing
Quietly to a gong.

This is the time of day
Patterns to die in, I
Wonder complacently,
Are not on top of me
As light longs into bye,

And each minute goes straight
Till slowly a lifetime that
I watch accumulate
Revises into what
The clocks let light at it.

Fantasy

A whole man, a half man, a fellow of shadows, all
Kinds of thoughts fold up in my brain this instant
   and
Much as my father's own movements imprecisely
Fidget across in the gesture I put out towards
Whatever it is surrounds me—who then is it?—
I find myself continually like a household,
An entire family squabbling about a joke.

'Let's print a newspaper and in a secret headline
(Who'll edit it? Who wants to be the news?)
We'll publish (but our dead ones cannot read it)
How burglars crept through a pattern (We were had
That night, remember?) then with a bang (the baby)
Opened our old safe hidden behind the chimney
(Who's interested anyhow?) I once watched
Thieves bleed and the king of witches. (These proofs
   are clean.
Correct them.) That's how it was. (The whole sky
   broke.)'

Nothing

They say the experiential
Zero is impossible.
The mind cannot conceive it,
The heart cannot believe it:
That mind meets mind whenever mind
Notions its way through more refined
Lacks of possibility;
And heart meets heart and mind and hand
Although it cannot understand
More than its own immensity;
That every vacuum known to space,
In spite of walls round emptiness,
Must let the heavens' swift particles
Meander through it and displace
Vacuum with vacillation.
But you, my darling, when we meet
It is in a dispassionate
Area outside all relation.
We speak and thus create our silence
Where passion's peace and passion's violence
Combine in an autonomous
State that is not between them nor
Explicable by metaphor.
I am the nothingness of us,
And you are me, and we are two
Demonstrations that nothing *is* true.

Advice to a Young Lady

Take heed at bedtime of the hardening heart
And, when the ceiling stoops on you, repent:
     You have no time to start
     Saying how well you meant.

The room grows small at midnight, far apart:
It is too small to hold your ideal love
     And in the hardened heart
     You have no room to move.

It was the others coming to depart
Who made room for you, gently where you went:
     Your life is a small part
     Of all the time you spent.

Alone at bedtime you diminish still
And harden to defend what grows more small
     With each defence until
     There's nothing left to fall.

Those who are restless as the sunrise know
That the night comes and we are little worth.
     They die, but when they go
     Bequeath us more than earth.

They wake a heroic company in their trail
And leave an emptiness where men may meet.
     No walls nor five-barred jail
     Keeps them aloof, complete.

For to such men the meanest animal
Can come as close and can be loved as much
As not the noblest shall
That you disdain to touch.

Words Made of Water

Men meet and part;
But meeting men today
I find them frightened,
Frightened and insolent,
Distrustful as myself.
We turn arrogantly toward one another,
Caged in dogmatical dazzle.
Our eyes shine like thin torchlight.
Conflicting truths, we dazzle one another.
Never lately have I known men meet
With only darkness, quite anonymous,
Perched up between them on a song no bird
Would answer for in sunlight.
I have watched carefully but never once
Have I seen the little heaps,
The co-ordinated fragments of muscle, brain, bone,
Creep steadfastly as ants across the planet,
Quite lost in their own excess of contraries,
Make signals, ask for answers,
Humbly and heavily from those they know
Are equally ignorant.

Looking about the streets I find the answers,
Thin blobs of light, enamelled price-lists, brawling,
An impatient competition
Between all those who all know all the answers.

I find also certain bits of paper,
Matchsticks, sodden or cracked or still with safety
    heads,

Cigarette douts and their empty packets,
And also water,
Water that is stagnant
Or water flowing slowly down the gutter.

I sometimes think that dead men live in water,
That their ghosts inhabit the stagnant puddles,
Their barges float with the gutter water,
That they are waiting patiently as water
Until the world is redeemed by doubt,
By each man's love for all those different answers
Dead men have dropped on sundry bits of paper,
From glances blue as smoke, now quite extinguished.

My womenfolk find these thoughts troubling.
Action becomes impossible: choice is impossible
To those who think such things.
On thoughts like these no man ever grew fat.

Marcus Antoninus
cui cognomen erat
Aurelius

The world is Rome; Carnuntum, on the Danube.

A man seated, a tent, three thousand tents, a man,
His skin sponged brown by the Italian summer,
Darkened by shadows and the sun of Egypt,
A face tugged out by winds of the desert, tight from
    sea-plod,
Contrary to innocence, and gentle:
The posture harsh; the mind alone is active.
Respectfully his, a boy at the back of him squats:
In front, a skeleton enters
(Epictetus, the wise slave, walks):
Then an Immortal
Staggering upwards painfully under
Bundles, for burden,
Of brown sackcloth wings.
The boy and the skeleton grin and are earnest.
That is their nature. His, the duty;
His, the decision: decide.

There is an army and an enemy,
And one in ten but from which century
He tallies purposes and hears them hold
Clamour raised upon clamour,
Rattle of armour, death squeals.

A mind, erratic within
His decent body, carries
Piecemeal a soul which cannot live outside:
Looks out and vanishes ahead of him.

The boy squats pleasant: truthfully he is blind.
The articulated bones are hollow and unkind.
That is the nature of things. His is the Empire.
His is the duty. Decide.

The boy, a curt word;
The skeleton vanishes.
There, instead of it, stands
(Alive in that curious negligent flesh
He fears for his own)
No master now but his quiet servant.
Words and an officer,
Words, and a name: it was done,
And the hum of despatches begun
Two secretaries scribbling, the couriers off,
And a cold walk in the camp,
And a hot meal, and his duty.

Two hours alone he must sit with the truth,
That bitter gentleman all made of teeth,
Listens to cauldrons and the clank of torture,
Screams from the innocent and the unholy:
Then hearing this he must resign himself,
Prepare himself for action and forget
Warmth, with its quiet
Noise of a woman
Who once breathed beside him,
Cold, with its quiet
Clink of his skeleton's
Vertebrae in him.

It must be done, and it is difficult,
Difficult while soldiers
Aloud about
Tent, bed and table
Query, quip, react
To orders given;
Difficult in his tent,
Difficult in his Empire:
It is difficult to forget and threadbare follow
The thin mind of a slave compelled by masters
To move through all of it without the world.
Beyond all this, he must not ask for comfort.
Others have owned the universe before him
And his destiny yet
Will, fleetfoot, overtake many.

Thus ends his meditation.
Noise, and the tent-flap opens.
Noise, and his name.
He must go out, go sit in judgement,
And he must not make haste.
He ponders quietly and asks quick questions.
Mercy must not itself become unjust.
This can have suicide, but that the gallows,
And one is loaded with new innocence.
He breaks a sword and pushes out in silence.
He had no right to judge them, but a duty.

Officially a banquet, therefore sit
Above the ambassadors and drink wine.
Dim memories recur that take time in
But must be battened or constricted for safeguard
Of his immediate purposes in war.

He smiles attentively. He makes a joke.
A long way gone, but not a long way back
To the boy squatting over difficult sums.
Politely he refuses, makes a promise, then
Singling his enemy confronts the issue.
His empire is about him. His, the duty.
But then go back, and he must be alone,
Prepare for sleep; and it is an emperor's duty
Not to be weary lest he waste his empire:
Barbarians, past the number of sleep,
Wait with long swords for civilisation to nod.
To sleep and not to dream, for in dreams too
Hordes gather against him
And against him bring
That sickness for slaughter
Which history has
Leached into his lineage,
The rattle of armour, death squeals:
And, in his bed, lean hungry longings taunt him,
Pinprick and bite him;
Deep dreams of goodness keep him from sleep.
Why have the heavens not elected him
To be impoverished, alone, unheeded,
Taken all from him but his own mind only
And given him freedom, made him a slave?
O Epictetus! Corpses are moving!
The slave he ambitions
Walks and with humble lessons
Proves the futility of all desire;
Fades in the act, accepting happiness,
The red earth round the oblong of his coffin.
Again the emperor shuts his eyes, and sleeps.
Let no scream from the tortured,
No prim innocence in the reprieved,

No cry against the cupidity of his time,
No pity for men in battle nor for his ancestors under
   the earth,
No lingering on the loveliness of the flesh,
No hunger after good honour,
Not a single prayer,
Not a hope of mercy
Corrupt the darkness in which he is resting:
Let him lie easily until the morning.

Then, to rise up, punctual not previous.
He puts on dignity like a suit of sack-cloth,
Walks in the weather that is sharp and sad.
He calls his commanders to council.
It is time to prepare
Another ambush.

The Transparent Prisoner

They took me somewhere sleeping in the desert
Up middle of a minefield near Benghazi:
And I was hungry—but that was later. At first
It was the Germans—you'd hardly call them Nazi—
Polite and battle-hungry happy men
—O I would like to meet those chaps again.

And everything was decent at headquarters,
After we'd picked our way out like with tweezers,
Decent and capable, and we were ordered
Into small companies, and fed or feasted
Better than back in Cairo. So for ten days
We waited, glad in the shade, glad of delays.

Then we were shifted in a desert truck
Back eighty miles, the sun like liquid steel,
The smell of heat, the nagging—until it took
A hard wrench on my memory to dispel
Those green and English places and the sounds
Which hiccuped at me, festering with old wounds.

But it was still the Germans, and one talked
At great length about his home-town, in what
I soon could recognise as Marburg—talked
And was glad of it, till I let out
A long throng of impatient memories:
Together we mourned the way of instant dies.

There was a Frenchman too—some sort of pilot
In an ugly bandage. The three of us
Got talking, all odd accents, and in a while it
Wasn't just words: we sang the Marseillaise,
The Land of Hope and Glory, and Auld Lang Syne:
Till on that note we reached a little town.

There we changed captors. We were back at base
With I-ties, or Italians, or plain Wops,
Who pinched our watches but could not refuse
To feed us on a diet of their slops.
And it was there that I first learned to sense
The tidy brutality of a barbed-wire fence.

It lay about us, rigorous as the proof
Of human ignorance finally seems to men
—A limiting condition of all life,
Not just of ours—though it was we alone
Who acted camouflage halfways symbol to
It—and the laws we're hourly half-dragged through.

Everything worked by halves, and half-alive,
Half-starved and half-imprisoned as we were,
We were half-tempted almost to contrive
Escapes across that rusting wrestling wire;
But we did not. Instead, half-hearted jokes
Tried to persuade us it was all a hoax.

Then soon it ended, because we moved again,
This time on foot, and I don't really know
How many miles made up the phenomenon
That I describe, though not remembering, now.
Miles anyhow there were, no lack of them.
And afterwards more miles, and still the same.

It was the desert and the sun was high
Or it went down; but it came up again:
A negroid Cyclops or at least his eye,
It pointed at us like an accusing gun
Which would go off if for a moment we
Forgot ourselves so much as to feel free.

Of course we had been guilty; so we went
On, though complaining, yet without arousing
Any emotion that was really meant.
We walked ahead, hypnotised by the horizon:
It wriggled in our sweat, in one round drop:
We did not reach it and we did not stop.

Then the night fell on us whipping us with sand,
The cold, the dry grains in our nose and nails;
The tickling blankets and the loud command
To sleep or wake or empty filthy pails—
—Words in an language that meant no more to us
Than to a bird the fumbled blunderbuss.

We could not sleep, nor wake. We seemed to touch
A secret manifestation of the truth:
We lay down in the desert, and learned to teach
Ignorance to professors: we learned to mouth
Old truths, and to forget them when they hurt,
Hurt us too much: truth became true as that.

We seemed like looking in a dead man's eyes
To see small stars dipped deep in the black pupil,
We'd suddenly and simply realise
How old astrologers could without scruple
Paste our lives on to them and advertise
Their rigmarole as wisdom to the wise.

For they were lying like in a black cup
Tealeaves made out of pure white light might lie
And formed a pattern, and a single drop
Brewed from those fragments of immensity
Could satiate thirst, it seemed, and let us pass
The ghost that most and momently haunts us.

What could have been the banquet of the gods,
I almost wondered, what could it have been
If these stars are the dregs? Are all men besides
Morsels to nibble when the feast is done?
I thought until the thought hardened past pain.
My thoughts grew eyes. They let the stars down in.

So for a long way: but it ended near
Tunis—you know the place. Most of us died
There—but you don't. You never will know where
Tunis pitted the map. It was outside
The squares they plant with pin-marks, beyond the four
Wind's quarters. I lived there. It is everywhere.

You'll reach it through a miserable month,
Sliding on sweat, cartwheeling over vomit,
Climb a few corpses and about the tenth
You'll turn about and think you've reached the summit.
That was your own one, was it? Not at all.
Here is another. You let your foot fall.

Daylight became a sticky mess of flies,
A filthy porridge stewing in our blood,
Lumpy with bubbles, and the rest of us
An ulcer, an excrescence, where they stood
Next me, a second; then they disappeared
And left me as before, and I despaired.

[46]

Starvation hits you innerwards like that,
Forces pattern on thought, on feeling, and all
We most think moral in man. It doesn't act
Only. It's something bigger: it thinks. And call
Yourself what you like, the image of God, the True,
Starvation alters reflection. It alters you.

And takes you down with it, through horrid slopes,
Along with shapes, and higher in your brain
It walks and wants, and everywhere escapes
Into its proper hunger, making the mind dim
Over—mere mechanisms built to try
New methods out, try, try to satisfy.

Starvation can lead you to Tunis—the one I know.
It is an old town. There men have lived
Since men have lived, and those who died there knew
That it could hold their bodies, and believed
Others would find a burial ground there too.
I lived there, all of me. Don't go. Don't go.

The stench, the itch, the dysentery, the hours,
And then the moment when the guards brought
    bread:
I took the lot and gobbled on all fours
And didn't tell them that my mates were dead
Till the thick smell of them and the discoloured face
Made it impossible and I ate still less.

Four men, a breakfast roll, a pail of water,
With at the bottom suds of macaroni,
At least a dozen but about as bitter
As the green slime that rots across a penny.
Hell has its comforts. Those who died forgot
At least the worst of it but I can not.

[47]

For life goes on. It keeps on going, going
Over the old hard ground, and the unbroken
Heart breaks again. I felt my life-blood slowing.
Death was at work; when suddenly I was taken,
A slab upon a stretcher, to a ship.
I did not eat there and I could not sleep.

Guns snored from Malta. Planes bounced above my
   head
The decks and port-holes splashed into the water.
Winds swarmed and hopes subsided. Thoughts went
   dead;
And hours went pounding hard and helplessly,
Like iron pistons into emptiness.
Then the sea loosened. We had come across.

And then they tended us, gave us to eat
From wholesome plates. We lived in an old castle,
And gradually our limbs at last forgot
They had been hungry. Lips began to whistle,
Fingers to hold a pen, and pain to go.
Thoughts bustled through us, hopefully to and fro.

It didn't last, of course, but nothing does,
And we enjoyed it, knowing it would end.
A train ran weekly and took some of us
Out of it somewhere but I couldn't find
A clue to the direction till one day
I was among the ones who went away.

It must have been two months between the two
Modes of starvation—one, the quick acute
And killing primary need I had come to know.

Death gurgled near it. . . It seemed a mere brute
Rampant and miserable, plunging with a moan
Its whole weight at me: in me like a bone.

The other—but it was in Germany—
A perilous pedestrian sense of God—
It lasted longer, outlasting sun and snow
Two winters and three summers. I watched the slow
    plod
Of overladen feet, till I had seen
Footprints like letters form an articulate line.

Or rather—but we lived in a tin hut
With one of those long reaches for a prison
Where the slack landscape folding out of sight
Seems to crop up again behind the horizon;
At least we slept there, when we had got through
With hacking coal for sixteen hours a day.

They kept us there for coal, alive enough
To cut it in the dark, but not to think.
They gave us porridge and a kind of dough
Half-baked to bread, and sticky soup to drink.
I ate it, gave them coal, two years and more,
And shivered in a blanket on the floor.

Any conditions continued long enough
Will stretch themselves until a man can live
All of him, in them; and the lowest life
Give highest impulse headroom, though he have
A hutch, a hole, a hill, to habit, and
Squalor alone to love and understand.

That is what baffles tyrants. Only death
Can end man's freedom to be all man can.
Prisons are perches. I went underneath
Then came up with a precious undertone
That swirled to song out of the damp dark
Through coughs that came with it and made it stark.

There were enough of them—incarnadined
The shining rock-face with thick frothy spittle,
And hours enough after the coal was mined
To watch how others bended or turned brittle,
Broke in a moment, and the hysteric calm
After the black barred ambulance had come.

Yet in the tunnel, at the rock-face, when
Accumulated by exhaustion, thoughts
Would form and fold and hold themselves close in
About the point of peace, were other states.
The shift, twelve hours had gone, and six more yet.
The pick-axe slithered in my hand like sweat.

Huge blocks and boulders mined off hours ago
Would seem a sick weight, and my stomach turned
Into a sob, and memories of snow
And footprints tapering backwards through it burned,
Like tiny monosyllables blaze, with fear.
My weak arms worked. I seemed to disappear.

Lying along my belly, the rock roof
Two feet above, the wet rock floor upon
My muscles sliding, I seemed to grow aloof
From my own body or to grow a skin,
Flesh, form, and senses, deep within my own
And to retire to live in them alone.

My hands against the coal would grow transparent,
Then, like a match felt softly by its flame,
My arms would char into a wandering current;
Warm radiance crept up them till the same
Vivid transparence flooded every part
And I could see the beating of my heart.

As sedentary worms that burrow in
A froth of sand cement it with a slime
Out of their own skin, I too shed my shine
On to the rock below me till in time
It took the same transparence as myself:
I saw its seed, its kernel, through the filth.

And then above, the rock like catching fire
Bled into clearness to the pointed grass
That bled beyond it; and the sun that higher
Winds in its web this planetary mass
Grew clear; stars stood above it, and ranged behind
Its brightness like the workings of a mind.

I saw the moments and the seasons swim
Precisely through me and I saw them show
Huts, hills and homes, and distance, and my dream
Of little footsteps shrieking in the snow
As they tip into darkness, all grow bright
And smother everything in transparent light.

I watched. A tender clarity became
That moment mine, as clear as through a hand
Bones shadow out into a candle's flame
And tender-terrible as to understand
Faults that the finding of has often killed
Pity and pain in you, fault-ridden child.

And I acknowledged. O I don't know what,
But greater grace than my acknowledgement
Could ever reach the edge of, or forget—
A tender clarity that would not relent
Till I saw mercy from the merciless brink
Of thoughts which no mind born was born to think:

A tender clarity that is not understood
But by the helpless in a dangerous instant,
A perilous deity. O my good God,
Come quietly at last, and become constant.
The years grow small about me. I despair.
Impose your order on my every hour.

It was an order, yes! but not imposed
Though not within itself complete, and not
Abstract—an order, movement, force, composed
Of situations, things, which one great thought
Transparented completely through its mind
To light long images laid down behind.

I was at mercy of them, am unable
Ever to meet except set in dismay
No, no, not shadows—but the implacable
Splendour descending, splitting tenderly
Skin, skull, and atom, till, though merely man,
I recognised a reason for all pain.

I saw the world, the world in full transparence,
Stark peaks through earth like vultures crowding
    down,
Become a symbol for its own appearance,
A system that completely and unknown
Was worked through by old forces and old laws
Which let it mean them, being what it was.

[52]

No other certainly. It didn't change
But stayed as still as in the stifled heart
Feelings not spoken, words would disarrange,
Can lie in hiding for their counterpart.
It was the world. Confuse no heaven nor hell.
The boring bubbling world you know so well.

The cold unclean and comfortable world,
Hard as an anvil, pointed, and as flat;
Circular saw, the orbit, square sphere swirled
Through bones, through brains; the spotted speedy
    spate
Of rivers, riders, racing with a will
Past men and mountains through the inexplicable.

Lying along my belly in the mine,
Or labouring footprints in the German snow,
I, the involved one, learned to love again
And, loving it, attempted to reach through
To the broad air, the people, though for years
My pit-prop prison peopled unawares.

I learned to love the self-same world as now:
For love of it, though its transparency
Was my captivity. I planned carefully how
To reach through to it and in it to be free.
I killed a man. I killed him and escaped
Into it living. Then, at last, I wept.

I got away through the Bohemian South
And into Yugoslavia where I joined
A band of partisans who lived next to death.
In that excitement, thinking was postponed
Or sharpened hard on the best ways to kill.
I kept myself alive, and that was all.

But now as years pass and the war is done
I find myself of evenings often enchanted
And, guessing what goes on within my brain,
Conceive myself as of a being haunted
By corpses more alive than his own flesh:
They dog me with a brittle tenderness

That breaks upon a whim, but nothing breaks
Through my continual sense of loss and sense
Of being cut off by simple slight mistakes,
Everyday errors, from an innocence
That is still mine though it lives a life apart
Folded transparently in the transparent heart.

Tree

Tree. Tree. Do you want to become a man?
A woman then? A wren in your branches?
You, tree, who stand stiller than I can,
      Do you want to move?
To flicker away from me, safely and swiftly away.
      Then slacken up to say:—
You are mine; I am yours? O tree, do you want to love?

You stand, tree, in the thick grass,
Upright, unquenchably still. A man passes.
But you, tree, stand still, and still as stained glass
      Gather the light
In a green bouquet, gather it up and spill
      Shadows about you until
With a dark splash like a beacon I wade in your night.

Then I look up, tree, from at your feet:
Sunlight splits into a shrapnel pattern;
Leaves become black and the black leaves meet
      In layers on air,
Tenderly frisking, yet stubborn under the wind,
      And stubbornly in my mind
Remaining delicate though your black boughs glare.

I think, thus looking, that perhaps gnomes
In buried places where they are homely
Must busily, when the sky becomes
      Top-heavy with light,
Lift you up chirruping to its zenith and
      Brush the whole sky with green land
Till it looks like earth, earth photographed in flight.

Or that the clouds, which frolic and glare,
And sly as a weasel, furry, unfearing,
Have let you down from their pleasant nowhere
And bundled you high.
Tree. Tree. Symmetrical bonfire, igneous green,
What did earth's heavens mean
When they let you fall then filled you with the sky?

You do not care. You'll not be caring
Whether or no it means that the queer
Energy through you is disappearing
With nothing more given,
That empty gravities from an empty earth
Are throwing themselves through your girth
Until they can connect with empty heaven.

Or, if you do, how can I tell,
From the greedy cell where I guard myself
And count the worlds of me that kill
Neighbours with nearness,
How can I hope to understand you, tree,
You, the arch-stranger to me
Who cannot reach my own articulate clearness?

I stand beneath you and you build halls
Like filigreed cobwebs out of valleys
Or over my head where the slant light falls
You spill your sheaves
Of garnered shade about me, changing its
Brilliance to brilliance that splits
Leathery, lush, an involved aether of leaves.

I, the supreme animal, I man,
Dream you up shapelier than the land
That nourishes you, or the sun can.
            I who create
A mythology out of your driest twig, who can make
            Your thickest timbers break,
I ask you to enter into my own estate.

Crouch your great body into this
Sweating sensitive skin, and listen:
These eyes watch, these lips kiss,
            This heart breaks:
But you, for all your gusty lunges, can't
            Even begin to want
The love that feeds you or the truth that takes.

You could have motion to teach you how
Nothing ever departs slowly:
You could have language itself to show
            Why hope must fail:
And finally, climactic in your mind,
            You'd know that you were blind
And other knowledge is impossible.

For I, as I stand sweetly here,
Look up at you and see you clearly
As one more thing I can't come near
            From above or below,
Discover you will never want to be
            Anything other than tree
And understand the thing I do not know.

Yes. I am man. I cannot wish
Anything other than my own foolish
Need to change shape and so to brush
    The air like you
And shoot long roots beneath me into earth.
    I deny myself rebirth
By wishing to be born again anew.

This play between us, you and me,
Proceeds by laws that bind us freely,
Me into man, you into tree,
    Together today.
There is a sufficient mystery here with you.
    Draw apart. We are two.
All this, all is sufficient. I go on my way.

I move away downhill over lawns
Where the evening buttercup looks like dawning
Into a warm reply to the songs
    I suffer by.
You shake your birds' nests in the twilit wind.
    You do not follow my kind.
You stand, arms open to receive the sky.

An Apology

It is the unforgivable
Essence of individual acts
Which uncontrollably attracts
Words through the incommunicable.

It is the story of a sin
Committed against our every dream
Of what we might one day become
Outwardly as we were within.

It is the story of a graph
Aimed at a bare infinity
But keeping in its inky way
Steadily to its paper path.

It is the story of a man
Who travelled far but could not find
One person whom he did not wound:
Until, deserted, he began

Making his shadow into bone
And on that bone put flesh of light
Which shone back with a passionate
Will to forgive him and atone.

Poem without a Title

It was so fragile a thing that
Suddenly we were afraid of
What would happen if it
Overtook us; and,
Frightened, we ran.

Then came a new fear that
Perplexed us, because we couldn't
Link fear with the beauty which it
Had brought near us, when,
Frightened, we ran.

We now knew only that
It had seemed terrible (but
Not because we might break it,
Rather it us); so,
Frightened, we ran.

Yet still more terrible that,
It being about to vanish,
Our whole lives should depend on it
Utterly. Therefore,
Frightened, we ran.

Later we learned that
Outside we could find nothing
Which would replace it, nor reach it
Within ourselves, though,
Frightened, we ran.

The Moth

The light browses, wading these shallow walls
As though it could be patient, but can not.
The light comes through and gradually recalls
Me to a place that no-one would have thought
Hidden within the manoeuvring waterfalls,
The trim cascades. The walls. The walls. The walls.

A death's head moth is fluttering in my room.

Darkness knocks at the window. I hear it move.
The light is trying to reach it but can not.
Land is outside, earth and the fields I love
And would be still as, but that every thought
Makes flesh a wall of water where lights have
Drunk and gone on. They move. They move. They
  move.

A death's head moth is fluttering in my room.

I follow hard on a whole herd of light,
And try to see by it, but I can not.
Only the walls, water, land, windows, darkness,
  night,
Impel themselves at me. My flesh and thought
Feel for a destination, but my sight
Meets only light. The light. The light. The light.

A death's head moth is fluttering in my room.

Sonnets for a Dying Man

I

To talk to you in all moralities,
Each to its true end mastered, till all one
Their intertwining helpful verities
Collapse across the gesture of your pain,
And then begin, replete in my whole tongue,
Each blind persuasion searched and hidden in
Its language luminously, at last begin
To tell you that, impossibly as you clung
To what you could not keep, what clings to you
Claws at its own ghost also yet to be
Created by your death, that though it try
To filch the pain which you are living through
It cannot take it: nothing can undo
The immortality of the day you die.

II

My children, come. Read in this book at bed—
Time of the times you cannot, and my dear
Procession through the uprisen words I've said
Hear of the fall at springtime from the year.
Loud though it buds, exactly to a head,
Springtime is time to hush and overhear
Perpetual ambush, treading on the dead
Spit of another springtime, disappear.
For to that fall it is I'll alter your
Words from the words uprising through my mouth
Unripened in procession: they'll fall for sure
When, and exactly then, they've said their truth.
Words of my mouth and children of my name
Come down from springtime, for the springtime came.

III

Break words with me: what little silence may
Still live in minds and minds communicate
That will I give you, or at any rate
The palpable image of what I cannot say.
Break silence with me: let the interplay
Of breath and breathing agonies relate
Another quietness to a better state
Than this slow parting will allow today.
At this breath taking let us both believe
What we have disbelieved, but not because
Of any terror or of any laws.
Let us break up all words that do not grieve.
But let us keep the truth, the truth that keeps
Us both alive when either of us sleeps.

IV

Not more than quietly that a loud land
Take back its thunder from a threatened sky
And you by heartfelt rigour understand
Why the grave dust should not be asking: Why?
But actual quiet yet, and a clear command
To wheesht away and hush each wild reply,
The eye that angered at the sight of sand,
The bones that hollered: Mud can never die.
Thus to accept: yes, quietly to have found
Life at the end of life by dying as
The least of things and least preposterous
Of the infinities that robe you round,
Not more than quietly let your loud lives lie
Down in the grave that overhangs the sky.

[63]

V

These words outdistance us. Voices run down
On slates that echo with the things we said
And splash new blood till chimneys streaming red
Beacon the traffic from another town.
The sun is in them and the damp clouds frown
Fertile from out of them upon a head
That, though it lives, can understand the dead
Who whisper in the sea and do not drown.
Not mine alone but many lives have brought
These words to life and live again as I
Search to return them to the simple thought
That will extravagantly multiply
Your life through death and ravel up the knot
That binds their utterance to eternity.

VI

Because it's here (out there arrivals spin
Identities beyond us) and it's now we feel
Throngs thudding out of water to begin
Quietness in us and we find them real,
Because it's here at last, and because we can't
Draw a breath nearer now it's reached us and
It comes here searching us, is off the scent
Of what in all ourselves we understand,
We're more alive for it, for learning how
It's come that long way from us to fetch down
Familiar vengeance, and it lets us know,
As best we can, what never can be known
And can't be seen until, now that it's here,
We watch it reach us as we disappear.

[64]

VII

This place has come to you. It's lost your way
And now, man-eating on their nightly scout,
Contours instead of colours set you out
Upon a map that bumps up to betray
Your stillness to you as you stand at bay
And hear the wilderness (or did you shout?)
Howl for a road to light it towards your doubt
Which it will have devoured before the day.
It creeps diminishing within you till
It is yourself and you, an open door,
Flap in the wind at nothing: sea and sky
Have disappeared within the earth you fill
Who now learn what you may have guessed before
You do not know the world in which you die.

VIII

From all your worlds with all their repetition
To the discovery when they stopped and fell,
Love was the unconditional condition
Of peace in heaven or of hope in hell.
This world has worlds which are its worlds apart
Where centuries prolong a summer fable
Into that inmost miracle of the heart,
The love whose listening is irrevocable.
From all your deaths all songs are lullabies
To the awakening when all deaths have gone
Down into darkness and the dark worlds dawn.
From all your deaths love floats its worlds, and cries
To you to follow by the million on
A fugue of footsteps of immense replies.

[65]

IX

Come into exile, prisoner, from the vault
Where memories draw your blood and the blood
   dissolves
Your features. Used as a butt, your every fault
Made critical hostage by your congested selves,
You, like a rascal's puppet, dangle on
Spurs, snakes, and fire. Cut into ghosts, your flesh
Inflamed, burnt hollow, your very mind is drawn
Apart, its thoughts taught tortures, turned to trash.
And yet if once Prince Exile call you home,
Your hopes his mild disciples, but your cage
Miraculously otherwise and rare,
Your rascal selves rally, and you become
Precious to them, and they revolting rage
Down hours and arteries to defend despair.

X

I close your door behind me carefully
And walk into myself upon your bed
In the thick street where the remaining sky
Skims the horizon from a chimney's head.
Rocks stuck together build up to a dome.
Snow scuffles off the main road under wheels.
You melt out bloodlessly and become the home
Of my own being till my blood congeals.
Men go inside the stones and disappear.
The roofs are white-washed, turning brown, like
   snow,
And as that goes this city too must go.
There is another roof beneath us here
In the man-eating landscape in your room
Which I will not leave till I reach the tomb.

[66]

XI

Your voice turns in me like a talking knife:
Your blood rusts mine: your bones have turned to
   teeth:
Your lungs inhale the remnants of my life:
And I am murdered by your whispered faith.
And yet I live, and you are still betrayed.
I'm more than anything that man in me
Who would forget you and who has arrayed
My selves against their own infinity.
Your enemy within me takes his turn
At talking. I am that man he'd gladly burn
And he is my accuser. You two meet
And with one voice you both accuse me: yet
You each know that as every hour was born
I stole my life to lay it at your feet.

XII

Keening away in quietness as best
I, the intruder, can, at your last hour,
When, being lost, you, by discovery blest,
Like an old pirate finding a new shore,
Lag, though outdistancing all that went before,
Upon a land beyond what you had guessed,
Within the body that will find your rest,
Far, far, behind the person that you are,
I recognise the stranger: I reply
Across the ghost at his occasional
Polite beck of the hand: I give you all
The things we give the dying: and then I,
Smoothing your sheets as quietly as I may,
Find that I've said the things I cannot say.

[67]

XIII

You who crop up between the world and me,
You the king gooseberry with the ace of spades
Who ride in silent riot as in raids,
If sores were weapons, Vikings rode the sea:
You with the snoop-looks, here to disagree,
Or spoil the whisky, sap the lemonade,
Or to dissect the corpse from an old maid
Who wobbles outdoors on a spending spree:
You who when most I want to be alone
Come interloping with one bottle more
Of bitter stuff that turns the blood to bone
And makes dust burn where muscles bulged before:
You who are dying of the life I live
If you can read these verses then forgive.

XIV

For all its rich bravado there's the skull,
Big bones and little, thick thin flat curly ones,
Fastened together in a poor white ball:
And underneath it lies the skeleton's
Facsimile of a man. Though the man can't
Cry any longer or deny the truth
This represents him, and for all its scant
Structural pieties he is this beneath.
The baffled mother scrapes her little son
Into a vase. The battlefield looks land
Until you notice blistered corpses in
Ditches, at back of dykes, half under sand.
The son looks up to see his mother frown
And caterpillars crawling through the skin.

XV

The old man dozed. The hospital quietened.
Nurses went whispering past his unmade bed:
While Mr Childs, who has no stomach, yawned
And those with papers put them by, unread.
It went all right till tea-time. Then the trays
Trickling like iron water through the ward
Wakened the old man and in prompt relays
The nurses gathered to be reassured.
The old man wakened but to what old tales
Of overwork or underpay or hate
We'll never know. By now it is too late.
But Mr Childs, who has no stomach, swore
The old man rose and tried to shout before
His eyes went slimy with the look of snails.

XVI

This, I suppose, is what they mean by death,
The senses clogged, the air inhaled upon us:
Your chest is snatched at, torn by your own breath,
While doctors search you for exotic faunas.
Fix the glass slide in flame, stain, and remark
That chain of streptococci under oil.
You look up like a dog that wants to bark
While they transmit your heartbeat through a coil.
Merciful monster, doctor with a serum,
Look at your own eyes in my instrument
And then correct your inferential theorem
About what death is, or rather what you meant.
All you intended was, of course, no lie:
Admit it though, you didn't *mean* to die.

XVII

The things our ignorance tries to reconcile
With a bright good imagined in the summer
As something of a spiritual tremor
Or in the winter as an icicle,
Remain in contradiction all the while:
For though there is the dream there is the dreamer
Who seeks and sucks from them his every humour,
Nor was the world invented by his smile.
It is hard fact and fertile with its proofs
Of what is possible within it and
Impossible for us to understand.
It is a rabble of self-evident truths
With no invention added, no demand
For a new meaning from the one at hand.

XVIII

Shadows are fruit let fall by the cramped sun:
Its permanent orbit, blazing pedestal,
Contracted by criss-crossing to a cell
In which we watch it prowling while we run.
We run to reach new systems which have none
Of its or our spry littleness. We call
Our lives out after us. They swell, dispel
The place they were alive in, and are gone.
That, of course suicide, is how we live.
In our immensities we disappear.
As if they'd struck and been quenched in a tear
Planets burn black to us which cannot give
More light than that we knew when from the sun
Ripe shadows rained hard on us as we fell.

XIX

Even as at first, when every world loomed damned
Over us, hang over, avalanche ready to fall,
There came Christ, and the Buddha came, and they
  calmed
Those they led inwards to a still higher hill,
So doubt redeemed us. When our experience
Made nonsense of itself and let us think
Each thought mere thought, it gave us a defence
Against the unthinkable, a blot on invisible ink.
The process was—we knew we could not know—
Different from knowledge. The world was our surprise
And when it came to peer into our eyes
We thought that we were learning, and we learned
  slow.
We learned too late. God, like an iceberg, was
Already neck-deep in our godless laws.

XX

The certainty in the forest wears a green colour:
Blue wisdoms rise from water: and the sky knows
Principles penetrating tall rainbows:
Man learns by doubt: his certainties are hollow.
The seasons also understand one another:
They keep to precedence and, though they alter, no
Quirk in the weather alters how they go:
If man finds means he makes his brothers follow.
Man's moral exactitudes never iron out.
Brainy vitality splits him open to thought:
Then skulls creep out like beetles and turn white.
His red blood's all the metaphor he has
Ever for certainty, and that he must lose
Whenever it is certain that it was.

[71]

XXI

High tiding anchors us. This world is never
So well away aboveboard that it lifts
Us beyond topmost and the dark spills over:
A talisman will hold us lest it drifts.
High heaven banks down at us. We shoal whenever
Its peaceful progress takes us with its gifts
Or heave up steadily till its ocean shifts
Our names for sure upon a solid river.
Not then away, skull. Hug the grave's earth, bone.
World wounds are bandaged by an unwinding sun.
Lie safe beyond all notion that your size
Mimics these infantile infinities.
Let me who have been doing and have done
Lie down beneath a low wall hung with cries.

XXII

Who the dead are or how to learn their habits
Remain not questions but mere nonsense spelt
Carefully out to us by the way we felt
When we first learned that we must die like rabbits.
Dreams changed to nightmare: now the mind
    exhibits
Reason perhaps, more likely panic, and
Corruption by an inchtape into titbits
Is all that it pretends to understand.
Its dead are joined by slipknots through the bone:
The pink lank worms have tied them idly fast,
Just as the reasonable live men guessed:
And if a world escapes it's quite unknown,
Since what has perished, having perished, is
Not matter subject to analysis.

XXIII

Is it perhaps a telephone unanswered,
A sun in trouble, or a star on heat,
The B.B.C. truncating bits of Hansard,
Or is a ghost howling beneath the street?
I do not know what it can be you hear.
I know that you are listening, and I try,
By listening also, not to interfere
With your supreme unshared perplexity.
What words can say to me the words have said
Out there where nothing happens since you are
No longer there for things to happen to
And there's no way of telling what is true
You cannot find me any image for
Our knowledge of our ignorance of the dead.

XXIV

Weigh anchor into windfall and lurch at last
Up the ribbed ocean, green swell and unruly foam
Combed back in curls beneath you as you climb
On keels in wool and what you're drenched in dressed.
Its purl or plain, its odd or even twist,
Takes your blood nevertheless away towards home
From a heart weighed up more heavy against its
    doom
Than ever that sailor in a hornpipe lost.
It's worlds away now that the heart's cable croaks
Down to its hold in coils, and it's underneath
The weighed-up world that you with grinning teeth
(Rib-bones for jersey, silence for your jokes)
Will plunge however wind falls, odd or even,
While priests puff prayers to blow your corpse to
    heaven.

[73]

XXV

What man will speak it all? What man is dead
In his completeness and with not a part
Of this stark world forgotten, but fit to start
An argument with the almighty figurehead?
Proudly his own, he might give God his body:
But his intelligence would, by trim statistics
In the emergency, be always ready
For any trickery in God's linguistics.
Who would let sheep judge shepherds? Who would
    say
Let only convicts sentence criminals?
Or the insane alone treat sanity?
Yet to what court is it that man appeals?
God—the good criminal, the mad lamb,
Who drowns all protests with the words—'I am.'

XXVI

This emphasis is older than creation:
That of the uncreate the most valued part
Tugs innocently onward till it start
Solidity from zero's desolation.
The earth pours flowers up that were nowhere sown;
Traditions peel away; and thoughts run free
From something earlier than their memory:
Absurd of course, but things become unknown.
Then the mind alters us, till in the end
Even a past foolishness can somehow amend
Retrospect into prospect: and when we die
We suffer intellectual agony
Foreseeing centuries in which to spend
The time we wept in yet have no tears to dry.

XXVII

Memory moves against from opposites
Attacking where we are; or it undoes us
Gingerly, by remembering what we lose as
The vectors of ourselves; and nothing fits
Safely without it, and nothing is beyond
Its reach to change, yet nothing alters it
Except by a diminishing from the complete
Past, the imperfect burial, the open ground.
Thus when we watch it as we watch today
Our eyes, employing shadows, see the sun
Dawn out in China, but we can't say when,
Since all occasions enter, all lights play
Their part in ceremonies we have never seen
And strangers dance explaining who we've been.

XXVIII

Time's acres kindled in the sort of way
That could not burn us back to what we grew
Into at once and always every day
Reached or remained or merely thought we knew.
And having done it what was almost burnt
Flamed and was burnt again, and we were taught
That what we thought was almost what we thought
Was a mere cinder or a phrase recurrent.
But what was burnt, that had gone black indeed.
So time took time to make our legions risk
Their own dark enemy, and the tinkling reed
Which says forever that the winds are brisk
Blew time out windily across our way.
Thus we were ambushed into what we say.

XXIX

All men and the majestic animals go down,
And worms die too, and the sea monsters die,
And girls and giggling children, king and clown,
All the old platitudes put on a dignity.
But we forget them in the impatient things
They fetch to memory, what they thought was true,
What words replied through questions: and death
   brings
Oblivion to the particular things they knew.
We can remember them but we know it's not
Them we remember, rather an artifact
In the convenient language of our thought
Pretends it can return them what they lacked,
A place in us, a world beyond memory,
A tenderness that loves anonymously.

XXX

To see the petrel cropping in the farmyard
Among brown hens, trying in vain to cluck,
Trying to rouse the rooster, trying too hard,
And cursing its enormous lack of luck,
That, or to watch it stalling over snow
Starved, as at last, its energies pegged out,
Its fluttering perishes, and it does not know
What water this is though it cannot doubt,
That is not all enough. Remember then
The black bird, white bird, waltzing, gale and all
Fetch, lunge, soar, paddle, with an Atlantic squall
Or semi-Arctic blizzard, until an
Immense sea breaks you and the gunwales grip
And one storm petrel rises like a whip.

XXXI

Burnt to a life instead and shaped in flame
Messages over the sea and waved up high
As signal soul and flashing soul of the same
Wave-drowning wave, a gashed and glistening ship,
You bend back waters under in a heap
And step above as steep as any dream
The unleashed magnitudes to a sunburnt calm
Waved up and borne within your blazing shape.
Burnt to a life the sea your hull shapes out
Of waves, waves hustle and sizzling waves and that
Tall breaker with a legend in its beak
Come snatching at you into the plunging sea-
    wrack,
Swims off beyond the perished and beyond
Swirling horizons and is never found.

XXXII

Call it by what you will it, but do not
Forget that for the first last time you are
Outdistanced by your hankering metaphor,
Ambushed by definitions you forethought.
Death, as you may apply it, takes the lot,
The drama, deeds, the full house, and the spare
Bedroom where somebody is well aware
Of the assertions that control the plot.
Do not forget that. It will turn up again.
After the worms have gone it will remain.
Though worlds turn round the dead men lie there
    still.
Do not forget your holiday in Spain.
That is a part of death too, and you will
Find that each moment's grown immovable.

[77]

XXXIII

Those flaming Christians with their hygienic rose
Tattooed upon the lavatory tiles,
Who bend the penis to a sexless pose
And think of childbirth as a sort of piles;
Those gentlemen with asterisks in their hearts,
Those ladies without lamps, those virgin ones
Who don't quite have the conviction of their sins,
They are the negatives where damnation starts.
It is not all in death: there is no end
To the sweating, swivelling consciousness of that loss.
It is in life: to die is to defend
Life by that loss of laboured nothingness.
Those who deny it, though they cannot live,
Possess, but finally, a life to give.

XXXIV

Evil we unequivocally feel.
It cannot be uptilted, emptied out
Of universes by a sunlit spout.
Remaining emptiness would still be real
And as completely evil. Dead men congeal
In scabs about it: the dying shout,
Their new wounds opening, that they die without
The knowledge that was their part of the deal.
I cannot comfort you. My sins reply.
I cannot speak but in a voice that smears
Evil across the music of the spheres.
You know, as I do, that I too shall die.
Silently then I may wipe out the arrears
Due by an animal in eternity.

XXXV

Goodness goes on between us but we don't,
Ambiguously though we try to, dare
Define it better than as everywhere
A careful discipline of accident.
It's just not in us now to know what's meant
By the perplexed brocade, the intricate snare
Made of each other's lifetime, which we wear
As an activity or an ornament.
These words go on as we do: hear them preach
Back over every argument to reach
The conclusion of their separate ways of speech.
What they are answered by is what they mean.
Somewhat like them, goodness goes on between
Us and the evil we had not foreseen.

XXXVI

You will not choose the good or evil way,
But rather truly, as the truest should,
Between two evils each of which is good
Discover what is necessary today.
You will not have the time to stop and stay
Daintily nearby till you've understood
Whether you are the diner or the food
At the long supper on the buried tray.
And yet when all is ready you must choose
From all you've lost which would be best to lose:
Then, having chosen, let the whole world die:
While you, wrapped up in it beneath the land
That rivers wash, winds drag, and roots demand,
Will trail your worlds beyond you through the sky.

XXXVII

Time is a trespasser here: that the dream survives
The dreamer and this dreaming, that alone,
Or that to waken means the dreamer lives
Although his dream were hollow as a bone.
Either the fable is immortal or
Immortality is itself as plain
A hometruth though of heaven as the brain
Can recognise behind a metaphor.
All the contracting and expanding world
That men make out of what they almost know
Cannot control the prophecies they heard
When shapes of children bickered in their beard
And women silently in choirs below
The cut trunk knelt and saw the dead tree grow.

XXXVIII

That numerous stranger dipped in my best disguise
Worms his way back over the green hills
Which winds have shaped from beaten miracles
And which old thunderstorms and wells baptise.
He cuts across it home. His light denies
The dark it boasts of, and his step fulfils
The courage of the grassblade that he kills
Dead on the spot he reaches as he dies.
All silence enters him but leaves no trace.
Who is that man who walks without a face
On less than water, on a single word,
On a mere air that whistles its absurd
Jubilant anthem in an elegy's place
Under the agony and is overheard?

XXXIX

Christ comes to mind and comes across the mind
And ankle-deep like stitches through a wound
Wades words through anger, and He steps behind
The meaning of the movement of the sound
That we had heard as silence. His boulder rolls
Gruffly across our thoughts. Our actions think
Suddenly for us, and the beatitudes slink
Like butlers towards us with His blood in bowls.
All graces air today in the long park
Grass grows more mellow, and our words decay
Into the mystery that we cannot say
As naturally as daylight turns to dark.
We are so close, the world has grown so wide,
That we don't know which one of us has died.

XL

At last to wish for, fear for what you will,
The world gone out of you and the bones come
Clean to their last supper at the long table.
They eat in darkness. They do not remember
What was their end nor how to count their number.
They let the spade's scenery seep through the hill
Into their marrow, not speaking a syllable.
They do not know by what slow road they came.
They do not even want it kept unknown.
The secret stop. Between the rock and bone
All is in frank silence. And that is why
We think of death in terms of eternity.
Changes obscure the dead but are our own.
They have no way of knowing that they die.

XLI

And now that the impossible is near,
And after lips, the flimsy hours cajoling,
And after eyes that counted and saw clear,
And before ears are deaf to death bells tolling,
And while the white sheet crumples into grey,
And while the hysterical relatives are kind,
And after having learned the things to say,
And before finding what there was to find,
Shall the calamity without a tongue
Trail voices down, or narrow in the brain
With subtle queries, or run amok among
Those thoughts now slackened by the fact of pain?
Or shall the man, emerging from the torment,
Break through it all and live his dying moment?

XLII

Dig oars for teeth in. Bruise the rippled hour
That takes you out to where the end takes place,
Then tug apart, by night and final hire,
Lifelong from destiny its half a face.
Behind it bone, and as you shed your wish
To outlast in your journey but in vain,
You'll hear sunshining welcome through the wash
Of the hot body and an hour in pain.
I knew my skull had crossed bones with the womb
(Break bones with teeth till teeth break up like bone)
And that my death was borne within my birth
(Come, feed upon the six walls of my tomb)
And though we prayed together I died alone.
(Lie down beside me and become the earth.)

[82]

XLIII

Dead man, live bogey, living man, I am
Myself an aching shadow, cast between
Corpse and an action; in syntax of the dream
A putrid metaphor for each other man.
Like him in this that I am not the same
But by my singular agony and smile
Distinguished from him for a little while
Although he is more like me than my name.
I've heard you gasping through another's face
In the next room to me, and what I heard
Was my own breathing stopping in your place,
And both of us were listening and were scared:
Yet neither knew that in the other's mind
Danger went out like lightning, pain grew kind.

XLIV

Loquaciously through your selfish agony
You spill out groans across your crumbling room:
Inflexibly emphatic as the tomb,
Silences guide you, for today you die.
Implacably in the right they could reply
When you howl mercy at their apron strings
That, as they take you, you took better things,
A privileged pensioner to your vanity.
Instead of that there's lightning at your door
And silent lightnings nuzzle nearer your
Imagination's bones where they lie bare
Or covered up in brightness worlds below.
A selfish agony is the last place you
Could have expected it—yet it is so.

[83]

XLV

Make after me the contrary image of
A man assailable by the least whim
And there impale perfected seraphim
Anguished by answers truant to their love.
If you have done this then the two disprove
The life of each if both must be the same
And if you give their cancellation name
It will be ghosts you talk of or remove.
Yet in that image if you study it
You'll find your own face written, and learn to meet
Yourself in the immaculate disguise
Of nobody at all without surprise.
Thus you will watch the eternal life awaken.
Can a ghost die? Or nothingness be shaken?

XLVI

The barrows foundered when the Christian priests
Removed the dead from banqueting by night
In the black belly where digested light
Powdered to nodules, rotted into cysts.
A God, they said, more glorious in His feasts
Than earth in any of our human dreams
Lives in a luminous silence that redeems
The best of men from being the worst of beasts.
And at His table anciently while each
New moment splits into eternity
And men learn all things that no man can teach
They feed on flesh that cannot ever die.
That flesh is His own body: for love it breaks
Up in the hand that takes it, and mistakes.

XLVII

Already as I parse your life away,
Coiling its ruins round my tortured tongue,
A man of ivy, saying what I say
Through the blown worm-holes that corrupt your
  lung,
You turn back quietly like a snake on me:
Two fangs edge living out of the dead rubble,
Bud to a bird and settle on a tree
Where double tongues proclaim that truth is double:
That I who die—as you, the living, know—
More of the life I have than yours I lose,
Have come to offer what you dared not choose,
By your death healed when by my own laid low,
Till through the lives that each of us has lent
Death dies in both and songs deny lament.

XLVIII

I promise you by the harsh funeral
Of thought beleaguered in a spun desire,
And by the unlatched hour, and by the fall
Of more than bodies into more than fire:
And by the blackbird with its throat alive,
And by the drowned man with his tongue distended,
By all beginnings never to be ended,
And by an end beyond what we contrive:
I promise you on an authority
Greater, more sure, more hazardous than my own,
Yes, by the sun which suffers in the sky
I promise you—that words of living bone
Will rise out of your grave and kneel beside
A world found dying of the death you died.

XLIX

The life I die moves through the death I live
Corrupting even evil with the lie
Of the undying towards eternity:
It lives in fear that is life's negative.
I do not want to go. I will not give
The death I live in to the life I die;
Or trust it will reveal what I deny:
And will not die although I cannot live.
'Take courage, singer,' say your silent limbs,
'You sing of silence but the song that dims
All songs, it washes you and me asleep
And leaves no rumour where a doubt can creep.'
I stop my songs, and stop beside your bed,
And cover up your eyes—for you are dead.

L

Love listens and redeems. It is the sin
Knocking at some outlandish door within,
Or howling without hope that answer can
Receive it into innocence again.
By love of little things great love's undone,
Yet love of great ones cannot but condone
The extinction of the littleness of man
Which is the source where his great loves begin.
Love hears the sin that is the sin of love
Pleading to be loved, and it loves the sin:
Love hears the hate and the hard words that love
Speaks to its enemy, the love of sin:
And love is silent: silently it streams
Through the continual uproar it redeems.

The Men of Now

Yet one more day more level in deceit
And the long green-springing furrows that plot in
my brow
Winding over prehistory over the street
In an uneven and half-hidden grandeur:
A sheet of sheaves, they corpse more handsome a
harvest
Than falls our lot among the men of now.

Yet one day more more loyal to deceit
My Judas springtime hears the streetline echo
With the kiss of my journey that hurries, afraid to be
late,
Afraid of the plunge of the mine, of the sob of the
well,
That deep underfoot might erupt, bury or veil
In ascending deluge; collapsing, might squander and
wreck.

Yet one day more and never nearer death
I wait and write. Remember this at least:
That one man running home was out of breath
For fear of the mines and the veins aligned in the
earth,
Their undiscovered riches waiting for birth:
Remember this, and try to be appeased.

The True Company

From that beginning which alters toward
Total stability and toward
Every beginning's alteration
Through its decaying assignation
The true company keeps its word.

Semantics now, being at least
As modern as old, it yet brings past
Us, as it passes, ancient weapons
To show us that whatever happens
Happened also to gods and a ghost.

The gods, grown weary with literal
Divinity, sneered, and, sneering, they fell
Into sin to find new versions
Of innocence. Godly abortions
Unborn, unsinning, took them to Hell.

Literally too, the ghost could
Frighten children and haunt a wood.
But now the only ghost is dying
Of believing in the lying
Claim it had made it never should.

Swords sweat and swagger as the true
Company continues through
Each alteration in superstition
And hacks it down to belief. Transition
Cannot alter what it can do.

Its word is kept, throughout the absurd
Systems religions it rushes toward,
Clean, meaningful, sacerdotal.
Through all changes it keeps the total
Stability of the exact word.

Epilogue

That death might not be casual,
Flick thumbing ash in the swish of a squint draught,
Lint pad for a bruise-eyed nation,
Bandage to blindfold memories that laughed;
That death might not be an empty flesh-felt gesture:

That hereafter might not be fed
With mutes mad and the sane ones poor and scared,
An asylum from single beds,
From the profane ignorance everywhere shared;
That God might not be a charitable institution for
    the dead:

I wrote these verses down
And left them and was gone.

THE GENTLE
ENGINEER

The Gentle Engineer

I

Then, taking the bit of his blood between those
  molar
Masses of nerve, his brain, thrashed from the sky
    An incipient energy,
    And trussed space into solar
Configurations of all time, above all making, among
  all
Cuboid or perpendicular planes or facets, all sorrows,
  all well.

        So to these tales
        The town stands up
        At intervals
        That cannot stop:
        And no room's here
        For a root's tip
        To stab one layer
        Of slate or concrete,
        No water to suck
        In the paved street:
        There is no way back.
        We, therefore, here
        Must search that dead
        Beginning, before
        Roots raised a bud,
        Before the planets
        Sundered, the first
        Fall of the sun;
        When hot rain burst

The intermediate
Nothingness
To mineral seed
That fostered us.

Before that we were lost, because then made
Out of a lack, even of atmosphere,
    From a dissection of zero
    Planted and pieced, perfected.
Yet the stallion stampeding into direction through all
    that is, never continues, leaving
Us daily less lost, more perilously absent, less
    neighbour to nil and more grieving.

    I do not know the gods.
    I did not reap gold corn
    With Ceres, nor with Herod
    Suffer infection long.
    Krishna was absent from
    Those battlefields where I
    Saw men and screaming women
    Die and die and die.
    Even in dreamy fictions
    Visiting angels never
    Gave explicit directions
    On where lay my law-giver.
    Now in this city here
    Limousine wheels revolve.
    An aeroplane is astir.
    War is a safety valve.
    A lady shares my settee.
    I'm liked by good-humoured snobs.
    A policeman prowls his beat.
    Smooth women guard small cribs.

A drunken scientist nods.
The poor die and the rich.
I do not know the gods.
Here there is merely much.

I, who've begun to lose my life already,
(I had begun at that first sundering
     Of nebulae to starlings)
     Might one day drop these tidy
Trammels off, and coffin make a cockpit of all no-
     where, might
Lose life to what no life yet has to die, and so keep
     godly state.

     The adaptation, perhaps, is new,
     But the old wish still drags after traces
     Of blood at daybreak, the huntsman's halloo
     Still sounds, his leathery hound still races.
     Busily we are scaffoldings
     Gauntly and gracefully inset where
     The planetary desert rings
     With hammer and song and the riveting fire
     That yet may let us be taken down
     To unveil unpeopled our quiet construction.
     So I make hope of bricks, and grin
     Past atoms at my skeleton.
     Yet with my sensible elbow, I
     Can feel the heated crowds, their kind
     Peripheral anxiety
     Prodding, perplexing, heavy, blind.
     O woman walking with your child
     Past the placard about eternal life!
     O gentleman long-since grown bald
     With keeping wolf and werewolf off!

[95]

O child, you cry in your warm bed
What would you do if as you spoke
Death's intricate abracadabra made
Your mattress fossiliferous rock!

Immediate masses interpose between
Our origin and end, and no root's tip
    Can pierce that dark for vapour,
    Condensing grains of stone.
We, who are further from zero than flowers, gapped
    up and off from that first dead
Beginning, nestle away from it and draw nearer to
    one another's warm side.

    Yet it was we built mountains into gods.
    The curriculum of creation invented by
    Our earnest ancestors, fits elsewhere with
    The facts we are Here this city gently
    Makes ghosts of them, and offices marry us
    Away from the appalling intimacy
    Lonely ones hold with what they heard of. O
        when
    Will Genesis, that chill song scantily
    Muffled for love or the nunnery, once more cling
    To the naked charmed imagination of
    The most of us? Nearer that neighbour than
    Woman or man can come, which made nought
        noun
    And, without pedigree, begot and gave birth
    To all that time contains but cannot comfort.
    Houses take turns to hide us from the clouds,
    Women from lightning, but their sheltering
        weakness
    Does not enchant the intruder off. Look,

Where the town stands up, cheerful postcards encircle
Grief the poor ghost, industrious schedules dig
A superstitiously obstinate wall against
The winter. Death like the seed of ebony
Comes from strange parts. But in the conscious heart
Lives on a wayfarer towards the other end
Who with hard footsteps and hoarse voice can leave
A genial blessing that is no reprieve.

II

Light changes. Standing on a sidewalk
I, under stars, an orrery, feel
Cold winter swarm possessively towards me, or
Hear from my bleak position its sound.
Roots crystallise. Their cell walls shrivel.

Hear too, a remote insinuation on wheels,
The deed, the speed, the fruit of metal,
One car that whispers gently by
To leave the snow that locks about my feet.

This is a street and that the moon
On its high stool knock-kneed
In oblong petticoats; a sheet of light
Left to drape over me as round a nerve
Is white fat tightly closing.
Overhead the blackboard in the sky is grey.

I, in an ignorance equal to
Each solitary potential's moving

[97]

From the periphery inwards
Towards the brain, I carry
Messages that I cannot
Understand or amend.

Snow only and no stars is what I see.
I hear a motor's snort.
And what I smell is dried-up ice.
I taste the nicotine in my own saliva.
Nothing moves for me to touch
On this hooped tightrope that is world but I.
So touch and taste me, see, smell, hear me, world,
That we may know each other and be known.

Light sags beneath the invisible stars. Clouds drag
Like driftnets, ready, heavy to haul, low clouds
Entangled in tall spires. The snow banks up,
A slippery furnace. Well, readily, I
Will go, if I must, across the sleek and snoring
Automobile-driven, I don't know who it's by,
Makes snow sulk over us, a purse of ice.
Maybe too I will still, if the white fall
    Accumulates to become
    My dream in telegram,
Take roads on broadly as a way of knocking
Lights up in a quick, perhaps splendid, moment
Doorbells can bring us from inquisitive boys.
But, as it is, and the distances make little
Of all my haste, I move alone in this street
And meeting no-one, trouble none.

At this time, however, and as I move, my eyes
Pick bones from houses and crush skeletons
Up in round tears and flat glances, fragmentary

[98]

Molars of an imagination. Polish me bright
Earth, mother, kieselguhr!
Polish my eyes, you scraps of a planet!
Winterly and essentially you are
An awkward spread of
Rockwork, roadwork, paintwork, work and
Distances where my always autumnal
Traffic can cross: stuffed schedules frozen into wax
Melt down to fruit; they drop; they rot.

Whatever moves moves towards its end to end
Meeting its own newcomer from the cold.
I cannot move towards where but whither from.
And that perhaps is why herein I remember
The stale odour of summer,
Dancehalls where men, the capillaries of event,
Small people in lipstick or
Lounge suits swell beneath
A saxophone's blue shudder.
Yes, that is why I pass
Places peripheral
To the capital.
Silence is central. Operations deploy
A continual person I am
About and against his own best calm.
I tether geese to these walls.
Contra barbaros ducent
Handbills, handouts,
Toothpaste, resurrection,
Only, all only, today
Pursued with the vigour of spring.
I cannot see it but I look at what.
If she could live that lady would be blind
(Who is my love, who has my love),

She whom I build from eyes
At every angle of head and body,
She whom I would, who would herself, see clearly
Past barrier and distraction
The quick of existence.
I convict her, a crystallising witch,
Of sackcloth and ashes out of her worms.
She is not there who does not therefore,
And only a corpse lies nakedly still while we watch it.
It is her bones that powder with my glances,
As I move down this street that cannot move
Toppling I talk, my projection sidling away from
Streetlamp to streetlamp. Like towards negative
An impulse in a nerve moves on a brain
I tackle my pattern to this stone street.
It does not move. My shadow vanishes.
Another action blurs those images.
And I move on a little distance, instructing
My shape on the sidewalk behind me
'Here you are simple. Here you can be forgotten.'
Yet somewhere I know that spaces are interdependent.
Dimensions do not die.
The schoolma'am moon,
A spinster with parched breasts,
A swollen blackboard and a countless sum,
Hold me up straight on guy-rope lights:
Or else, unsteadily,
The outline of a head
Will rock over phenomena
And burn its lesson on stone.
I will not hence who will not henceforth.

Then at this point of continuous passage I learn
How action, the plausible vagrant,

Will not be stopping tonight,
Will not be stopping.
I see men sliced into hands.
They are locked in a purse of ice
And their disembodied activities
Roam in a noose or whirl
Winds against cauterised walls.
For when I move, the distance moves beside me.
The distance moves, the separation stays.
I am in this street. I move on the capital.
But though they lead these streetlamps cannot follow,
And though I move I cannot stay behind,
Perpetual as they would seem to be.
The fat man Space and his thin brother Time
Travel in my compartment, and I know
The cards are stacked against me. I will lose
An eternal soul to those continual thieves.

The roots go down that they may up again.
I am in this street. I move on the capital.

Polish my body with sandstone fretting, and with
Arrows fermenting from
Windows onlooking
A glance in love of this night,
Make it serene to consummate torture and
Remember the sun,
The mincing sound of water
With waterhens in the evening of moods once my
    own.
Hurdling synapse, that memory makes translation
By difficult language inform
And evolve itself into

The signal I see in the smile of a strange young
    moment.
Not action, but reaction, wisely then.
Remember the sun as it was,
Back in the summerlight.
This street of stones reacts to that memory.
The moon casts down flat brilliance.
Arid turbulence falls apart
And a belligerent mass
Of the silence in this street
Intrudes with its clean perspective
Over me,
That through me, by ecdysis,
In dropping of masks,
As dropped-off leaves,
The skin come clean away,
The five roots of the tree of knowledge vanished into
An ultimate focus,
There may be sympathy and my acceptance,
Loving this gaunt good street of stones like sunlight.

Let me, as orrery, be lightened towards
The insinuation of eyes that have seen shoals
Of the resurrected into tranquillity moving
Towards destinations that they carry on.
Polish my speech. Polish my words, you winds,
You undulations of sorrow, O scrawny street,
You bricked-up chimneys, abrupt clangs of a tram,
Teach me to speak, you exact observations.

Moving out down away far towards
Whatever capital you lead me to, I'll carry
As the thin nerve-cell to the brain and sinews
What you make into me of your own nature.

Long fingers of light, or is it
Chalk? powdering up before me, as the moon
Scribbles her giant handwriting across
Roofs and the dark grey sky,
Open my insight to
The elements of direction.

To move, yes, never away but always towards,
That is my destination.
Distance unravels within me. My taste buds surprise
Odorous sauces wrapt in the tang of a snowflake,
A curt rough brittle snowflake.
A gentle contagion alternating
Upwards through barriers energies spin
Correctly around the prisms, pinacoids, domes,
Each of its crystal facets, and around
The liquid walls, dissolving roofs and rafters
I am made up of, by strange architecture,
Infects us both, this crystal and myself,
With all the history existence has.
Immense intrigues embroider this instant with
The reactions of eras; pterodactyls lumber:
Ancient limpets are embossed on rock:
An oceanic sludge creeps into life:
The principals of matter find each other:
This flake and I converge from all beginnings.

I move across. I am made up upon
At every instant by a ton of bricks,
Cement and polished sandstone, granite blocks.
And fossils spun from powdery chalkmarks burn
Beneath my eyelids in the cold white night.
It is my own blood nips at every pore
And I myself the calcified treadmark of

Process towards me:
All of a million delicate engines whisper
Warm now, to go now
Through dragnets of tunnels forwards as my life.
I carry that which I am carried by.

It is this street at last has rubbed the layers,
Those static concretions of eyes, an observer's,
And wrinkles flattened, the mock objectivity,
So that I meet in my least, impoverished impulse
Enormous autonomies I come to dread,
And then accept as each involves away
Uncounted interdependencies in space:
And in my roots like sweet quick sap
Knowledge comes up through capillaries of reaction
And I know not what it was not I knew.

Eyes slacken. Words go down.
My seven senses yawn.
An old man, tardily
Past need of them, I
Am the skulking ground of tarsus, foot, hoof, wing-
    tip,
And dinosaurs with cobbled heads, their legs,
Crawl out about me to become my witness.

It is like death to lose thus the dear body.
It lies, a tangle of insidious knowledge
Across this traffic course.
I knew a girl, and with her warm wet mouth
She kissed a corpse awake,
And when the corpse with open lips assented
And hard hands held her and
Her head went back, her head went blank. She loved.

[104]

She has a house of level grass and is
A lesson on geography, unlearnt.
And that is death and that is what comes down
At every turn from stones I move among.

For I no longer know who moves nor why
More than my nerves know what they tell my eye.

This is a street and that the moon
But I do not know how nor when.

A maze of energies, dextrously from a dozen
Planes, planets and pinacoids swivel at once.
I carry on, but what I carry is
All these to where I do not know they take.
Distances whisper like a sleek motor car
High out ahead of me, and will not stop,
Will not stay steady till they are attained.
No action is possible. Only reaction permits
Untidy wisps of direction to float out.

An impulse in an enormous
Structure of round white light
I spin off through it at
The touch of rock, the touch
Of this street, against and over
And off through it towards. . . .

The moon watches,
Peppery, livid.
And action will not
Be stopping tonight.
Action will
Be going on.

Action will never
Come to rest
Nor ever be mine
By my own act.
The centuries go on beneath my breath.

The moon shivers as her bare white arms
Dangle uncertainly down between gables.
I cross the road, quietly underneath,
Towards the warm width of a wall in the cold night.
Lights waver off on either side. My shadow
Bites the black asphalt from its sleeve of snow.

III

'Hello! Hello!. . . What's that? of course it's me.
I got your telegram, and really I
Just don't know what you hope that I will say. . .
What's that? Don't say it then?. . . But Mary, Mary,
I must get this across. I must sincerely
Try to get over to you that he's why
I'd sooner shoot myself than have you marry. . .
It's not myself. . . It isn't isn't me
I'm looking after but I know what you. . .

It's absolute spring madness. Why not try
Pretending you've lost money. I'll guarantee
If you were broke you'd see him wince away. . .
I don't care what the weather's like. I know
About him. Don't put me off. . . O darling why
Pretend to happiness? You know I know. . .
Shut up! Shut up! Can anything I do
Ever get through your silly skull that he
Breathes up and laughs and coughs dishonesty,
Fat splayed cupidity, a walking lie,

[106]

Dumb cluck, a deadpan scrounger, any way
You find him out in. . . Hello. . . Hello. . .
    Goodbye. . .'

IV

Who then are you
I hazard after?
Are you my love
Who have my love?
I cannot yet decipher you nor disprove.

Where do you lie
And what between
Us launches this arrogant
Atmosphere
Through which you penetrate like a pointed prayer?

I come to you
Across across,
I come to you
And will be seen
Though five ambiguous senses blaze between.

Just as the sun
Goes up and down
I come to you
Continually
Whether I circumambulate or climb high.

I move, I move.
I do not know
Where to nor why
Nor how except
That you are ahead of where my last step slept.

This wooden table
And this blue pen,
Tarmac, macadam
And turnstile are
On which your treadmarks glitter like a scar.

Waysiding with
Fellows and fools,
Or sidetracked by
Intelligence,
I come to you. I come through my ignorance.

In Arctic seas
Slack waters push
My path aside,
Yet I move through
Waves from far underwater and come to you.

My toe-tip on
A stiff arête
Topples a stone,
And as it falls
An echo of it murmurs. To you it calls.

A prison may
Cloister that noise,
Round four lean walls
Its echo grope,
But you, its audience, always interlope.

Down roads that I
Did not prefer,
Through rooms I hate,
Past doors I close,
I come to you for sustenance and repose.

[108]

My shadow swivels
Drunk and remorseful
Into the night
Against the kerb.
You are its nurse and you soothe it like an herb.

When I am divided
Into my last
Small share in the world
I have come through,
I would be broken like bread and come to you.

I come to you
Across across,
Across the street,
Across the years,
Come closer each breath as each breath disappears.

Along the edge
Of oceans and
Along the hedge's
Decorous side
I walk away out towards you and you abide.

Elusive and
Yet constant to
Constant pursuit;
To you, my remote
Last love, all my love that lasts, I must devote.

I cannot see
Smiles in another,
And every tear
I brush aside
I find you hidden within it like a bride.

[109]

Were you stargazing,
A shy ripple,
Facing the sky
You reconcile,
I'd come to you in disguise as your own smile.

Or were you moved
Against the mean
Earth we are made of,
I'd be the hand
You hilted anger with and your reprimand.

For where I go
It is I am carried
And the why of it all
Is you understand,
You my direction till you become my end.

Gently you make
Me move away
From whom I am
I was I will
Become, and gently return what I fulfil.

An obscure construction,
My final title,
Made to move
And carry the years
By law of you, a motley of engineers.

Yes, gently you,
My destination
Describe and limit
My life of loving
And listen as I come through the noise of moving.

I come to you
Across this painful
Noise of my journey
Without a wreath.
I bear no grudge nor cargo. I carry death.

You will surprise
Me at the last.
We two will meet
Where no sun warms,
I, murderer with my body in my arms,

And you with me
As I at last
With you, alive
Past apprehension,
The dizzy annunciation, the slackening tension.

Biography of an Idealist

The Crystal and the Shadow

No wise humorous man
To light a frowning pipe,
But somewhat pedant-lipped:
Too thin yet over-ripe,
In thoughtful candour he
Stood an inch from the Throne.

He didn't like the king
But thought it cruel to kill
Unless, of course, there was
A matter of principle.
He knew his mind and that
Saints are a shabby lot.

The law was not for them,
The human dispensation;
Unwholesome justice or
Mere moral sanitation.
Saints could not be condemned
By systematised sin.

Their dreams were all exact
Replicas of Love,
Creations of the Creator,
The labour of the Dove.
No thought of man upset
Their regent symmetry.

His radiant mind performed
Its intricate perfections,
Illuminating summer
With brilliant bold rejections.
Childhood pursued him with
Ascetic ferocity.

Yet old enough to know
The bitterness of not
Distilling what is best
Out of the least thought
—Because there was the king,
A distracting energy.

A saint's shabbiness dresses
Gutters and colonnades,
And bustling stock-exchanges,
And the bare Queen of Spades,
Annoyances and sorrows,
Brash friendships and lush quarrels,

All are dressed in white
Patterns of dentilled silk
By men with lice in their hair
Who live on a diet of milk:
And yet the king despised
Rags, ulcers and bones.

He knelt before a monk:
I never quit this place.
A hermit answered him:
The mirror burns the face.
All night the stars were dark.
Dreams perfected his heart.

They came in harmonies,
Their courage crisp; they came
With tabors, flutes and drums
Brocading their acclaim
With wild handclapping of
His regent symmetry.

They came on stilts or, dwarfed
By insolent windmills, came
In figure S processions
As agile as a flame:
They came out of the black
Night of his white pillow.

Dancing, turning up
With ancient cut-throat facts,
They bargained hell for leather
That the damned might not relax:
Limbs were lashed to the dance
With sacred cow-hide.

Their motley measured mind's capacity
    to defy
The shades of startled lightning
God fastens in the sky:
And when thunder followed
He knew the time had come.

The king was counting money
And heads of corn and men,
Thinking the matter over,
And counting them again.
His tally was a small
Part of the passing world.

He knew the time was wrong
Although as right as rain,
As right as rain or thunder
Or water on the brain:
He counted out his money
And counted on his men.

Their weaknesses he knew:
Poverty kept him awake
Arguing that he had
Enough money to make
Their imperfections serve
His own imperfect ends.

The king surveyed his kingdom,
Following paper clues,
Historical documents and
Clippings of recent news.
The king frowned at his ledger.
His shadow danced on the wall.

A shadow's colour is
Inconstant consistency,
Half made of shape, half light,
And all transparency:
A shadow has the form
Of a very cool mirror.

The king was quick to think
Of evil in the wall,
And evil cancelling evil;
But the result of it all
Was still as evil as
Evil ever was.

The king was quick to learn
That what his shadow did
Expressed his best intention:
He therefore never hid
Within the light or ran
Away from his own shadow.

The king encased in light
Watched his shadow grow
Under the stern sunlight
Or in the lamplight's glow.
The king frowned at his ledger.
His shadow danced on the wall.

But someone else was watching,
Hidden within the light
Of his knowledge of the shabby
Soul of the king that night,
In thoughtful candour he
Stood an inch from the Throne.

An universe in crystal
Implored him to imply
By his ideal devotion
Its regent symmetry:
God in His heavens fertile,
Lightning lashed to the sky.

Lightning without a shadow
Yet not in a vacuum,
Completing the crystal's
Equilibrium,
Solidifying light
In every solid body.

Even the crystal dark
Lapped shadows from the lake
And obscure constellations
Groped about to make
Absence achieve perfection
In the blackest art of night.

Illuminated by
The inside of a dream
That casts no shadow and
Only an ideal beam,
The action in the crystal
Penetrated the brain.

'Now, king, the time has come.
The saints you scorned are free
To establish in your kingdom
The regent symmetry
Of man to man that is
An image of God's body.

'Prepare to lose tonight
Substance and shadow and
The sleek and timid falsehoods
You used to keep your land.
The honest worm will nurse
Her young at your breast-bone.

'You've changed the laws of man
And made the laws you break
But the Law of God will never
Alter for your sake.
Your flesh will decompose,
Your soul disintegrate.

'A man of bits and pieces,
Believing this and that,
An athletic ventriloquist,
A spiritual acrobat,
Your fall means that each thought
Will burn in a separate fir.'

The king looked at his shadow
As it swung round the room.
The king looked at his killer
And prepared to meet his doom.
He coughed to clear his throat:
'Ah, so at last you've come

'The years have been too long.
I can remember when
I thought your saints at least
As good as common men.
I should have died before
I lost respect for them.

'Perhaps I am unfair.
I die a usual death.
A traitor must be friendly
And pretend to good faith.
For myself, I never was
Above dissimulation.

'If I believed at all
I believed in the small mistake
In judgment or behaviour
That only men can make,
The perfect limitation
Breached by imperfect power.

'My evil cancelled evil.
Your good will cancel mine.
The limits of a shadow
Are difficult to define.
But the meaning of a maggot
Is that it has to dine.'

They led the king away.
They shot him just as dawn
Was beginning to cast long shadows
Over the royal lawn.
The saints were counting money
And heads of corn and men.

Ideals that grow like crystals
Concentrate energy
In parallels and prisms,
Contracting fluency
Into the symmetry of
The soul's geometry:

The soul that casts no shadow
Indicates human grief
With intricate lightning: but
God is beyond belief.
The shadow in the crystal
Is that there is none.

The saints are counting money:
Merely regent now,
Lopsided without shadows,
They cannot tell us how
The king within the mirror
Came by his pious gestures.

God is beyond belief:
His image everywhere
Half made of shape, half light,
Establishes despair.
The saints are counting money
Because the saints are men.

To Marie

But still and all the same, and as still as you were,
Through more than ever woman was born to bear
My verses marry you who are my wife
As partly mine as all I have never known
And as complete as any bit of stone,

As distant as a dream, but as near as one too,
As impossible as this if it's that which is true,
As good as gold, as better as blue in the sky
As old as seed, as best as the heroes who die,
My verses court their energy in life.

As deep as algebra, with exactly the same grace,
As general as sex, as alive as a face,
As intricate as death, but as simple as faith
Moving no mountains, moving the earth underneath,
My verses search for life in symmetry.

As slothful as a snake and almost as sudden
As agile as a boat, but solidly wooden,
As clean as sparks, as cold as the eyes of a child
Whose hopes have been betrayed, and as sad and as
    mild,
My verses court coloured energy.

Of Iron and Ice

I

At the table I tell in a wise warm truth towards
  sunlight
    Of iron, of ice.
Here men at work, the shoppy costers, flourish,
The dream is dug, the deed has ceased to shovel,
Departure is all around! O I could sit
    As desolate
    As locusts leave
Egypt its farmyards, beasts unburied bodies,
But that at the table, my iron, my ice and my lucky
    Magic at hand, I can listen
    To noises of gentle precision.

II

This freak of time, this callous clear defeat
    I cherish most,
I murmur with the resonance of iron
Vibrating after gunshot, and I dance
Through spectra that the sun shines into ice.
    Small bulletholes
    Dig me my wells.
I drink down thirst. Time waits at every turning
And dead hands clutch the used and useless iron.
    It can be melted down.
    Time will begin again.

III

With the heave of steel, small heartbeat stripped to
   an echo,
     When will you answer?
As naked, as gentle, as shivering, child, by the hour,
I carry my kings, voice in plain elegy.
Winter they won. Their perched battlefields toppled,
   Rivers and hills,
     And their smooth cold plains.
Their iron is all at a dead hand. Their iron
I sing. At the turn of the clock, O narrow boy:
     I take you back to my voice.
     I take you their answer to death.

IV

At the throb of the steeled-up heartbeat, the echo
   aloud,
     In winter I went.
Do not remember. It is not my going
As always into ambush. It is past
All fret with us. Time waits at every turning,
   Heals and hardens.
     This fight was lost.
Winter with thin partitions of gay ice
Sheds off a country rainbow. Here and now
     I watch the dead awake:
     Take up my heart and walk.

V

I move my words. I do not understand me,
     —And who would dare?
A tilt of knaves, I litter this sad varnish,

[123]

O quiet kingdom, and the roads all steel.
O messengers, your spry set stride, your clinking
    Errands of blossom,
    Hasten, listen,
Hard is the way back for the mayfly, hurry,
The sky caves in behind you like a tunnel.
    My heart cracks into crests
    At the fetch of your small squalls.

VI

Iron is wheels, is such a web of girders
    Round plaster rooms,
And gunshot is complete. I had not thought
But time could find ways through them, yet that I
In all a trice of tender pressures, phases,
    Made me my entrance,
    Never hoped. . .
Old narrow-chest, you were so young ago
I scarcely could put music on but cries
    Against bars used to battle
    My heart to a dry beat.

VII

And that strange distance in its coat of summer
    Mad March winds tailored,
Her lips were of a furnace not my own.
She such my love. And out of it what ice,
What clumsy crystal's separation comes.
    O narrow boy
    Remember her,
Take note, as the table turns tunes from the sunlight
  today,

That the king at our crest from his ice-blue whiteness
     may echo
          With resonant gentle precision
          Across that crystalline cliff.

VIII

I believe the bright kings perhaps we carry under
          That are in silence.
I have come close as earnest in wherever
Cause is disputed. Here the dream is dug.
Go down with them. Theirs is another iron
          But as efficient.
          Twin lines of steel,
And alien, yet at meeting in the eye,
Around their marriage grassblades tangle shelter.
          All distance is immense.
          All parting pitiful.

IX

As a crucible passing the pollen of test and denial
          I offshoot in flame.
I am all steel, all porcelain, all glazed,
And meetings and departures trade against me
Grains of my body. This is where I stand,
          As barrier
          And meeting place,
As ancient, and more than line nor likeness can
Unlean or disinter. And here I say
          All distance is immense,
          All parting far and fearful.

[125]

X

So the suspicious angler for his ego
    Might look down subways,
And the start of fish, their warty, wooden eyes,
Their trembling torsos, turn them to bait him back
To an outfolding answer, catch. Once more
    That moment lapses
    And the past happens.
It is here I stand. And here is no
Sure ground. I say believe. Believe in steel
    That rolls the rail ways home
    And undoes accident.

XI

I would undo the murmurs of her hair,
    Drape them aghast
As sinusoidal message. I would hark back
Before the hangman's privilege of murder,
Back to the latch laid indoors, and the room.
    Old narrow-chest,
    That journey waits.
It needs steel contours. It needs wheels and hills
And violence and the love, for man and man
    And woman, man and infant
    Scream in that great wheel's spin.

XII

I say as I tell in the easy light of the sun
    That there is onwards
There are colder climates, planets before
Our time. I tell as I say it of sundown's sharper
Than civilization's ebony frieze, of tongues

[126]

Turned woodpecker turtle,
          Of flowers in brittle
Broken words, of a scene in a setting of trees,
The woman, the father and the child they loved
          Obeying perhaps the bright kings
          Whose hearses I fever to touch.

XIII

Here, as naïve of statement as a quicksand,
          Time takes me under.
Shelter! All man is made of wounds. Bandages
Swim for his blood. The wound dances. All
Man moves. The bandages are alive. Alive!
          O woman now
          So much apart,
A part of me apart, here wounds wave up,
The dream is dug, and I am shipped in linens
          To warfare this blood through,
          This gap between us now.

XIV

I will uncover to the ice and iron
          Some strict swift level.
I will river time, bridge it with roads
Across the blood gone back, make use of even
Winter, and make haste. I will build you a boat
          As lovely, my dear,
          As a berry, I will build you
A bridge that will field you the past for a plaything,
     I will build you
A sledge that will cross you the red blood truly, and
     then
          I will watch while you're carried across
          Some ocean I had missed.

[127]

XV

Watch you, till out of sight I watch the wind,
      One way out further
At a game of icebergs, fields not my construction
Can quite ungate. All, all too open, and
The icebergs topple, a sudden malediction
      Like event.
      I will turn again,
I will turn to the iron in blood, all the crisp air
It holds, its sad deft journeys. I will turn
      Away from the sun like a planet
      Or a man who has watched your eyes.

XVI

Of such as sudden death has taken twice
      I'll audience.
Twice-buried silences applaud my mimic's baton
Past a musician's elbow crowd the notes.
And steel, and steel. It is all steel I sing
      Upon this bored
      Bone pedestal.
The organist picks his way home. At the street
   corner
Sobs on the spiritual soap-box, His day be done.
      But my bridged-up arteries roar
      With the pressure of vapourised ice.

XVII

All screaming roads, one perfect thoroughfare
      Takes silence onwards.
Its cargo human, and out of the drugged assembly
Coupling buffers glide. Their autonomy

Is unfixed. They are individually nothing. Only
    The silence they hold
    With its ebb and its throb,
Its capacity to be dragged by the pleasures of dusk
And its inert wisdom prevails. They really submit.
    They take time in. It is tame,
    Relinquishes and relaxes.

XVIII

At last it is meeting I mention, to tell of sunlight,
    My only end.
I lock these words behind me. I am gone.
This beautiful morning settles down like a vagrant
Upon the park bench. It hunches, yawns,
    Lies down to sleep,
    And few hours pass
But each that does, its whiskers waxed, official,
Sees it, stops embarrassed, and then, somewhat
    Lingering towards casual,
    Strokes the poor boy's gold hair.

XIX

Two pale worm twins whisper in an asylum.
    This is at evening.
In the next room, a giggling rattlesnake
Cajoles the moon to music. All night moves
Its blue hair pinned, 'small brooches' say the stars,
    And dance and dance,
    All distance toppling
Between their little arms, crushed and collapsing,
Their bodies pinned together by a planet:
    And for such love their way was
    The rattlesnake has died.

[129]

XX

Then the war-damaged, then the glass-spiked eyes,
  Then the departures,
Funerals and feasts. Through what strange laws
They came to each man's own? From what strange
  place
They came to each man's home? By what strange
  knocking
    O by what?
    And wherefore? who?. . .
There was a prison and a nunnery,
And in Hell's kitchen thinkers who were thought of,
    And when all these met these
    For what strange promise died?

XXI

Believe the bright kings whose intricate armoured
    Batallions beat backwards
Beasts of the powdered birthmark's pyramid voice
That a rail there is and a pioneer in metal
Who will hound down a home for those who come
  clutching us closest.
    Carry the dead
    Back up on a heartbeat
And do not envy their powdered well-wishing profiles:
They have their ashes, their monotonous triumph
    And in dear earnest it tells us
    We cannot know if we love.

XXII

Iron is wheels. Those dead in their circular systems
   Of sorrow and steel
Catch up beneath our breaths. My woman, where-
  fore?
Their all long lines of bones but of what brain?
Believe them, the perished, they have no new love to
  speak us.
     Reflect in that ice.
     Admire in that coldness
A creature complete as the grass because mixed as it
With the salt subjections of stone, the stone and the
  water,
     The mineral riches of earth
     That is silent and needs no souls.

XXIII

Let us move then, away then, meeting, recurring,
   O warring always,
As creatures of tempest and steel, the old ruse rising
And bringing back up from the centuries where
  they summer
An Egypt of kingdoms of lovers we love no longer
     But mix in as ashes,
     Are held by, relaxed,
And at last so surely reduced to a single existence
That only what we now call love is easy
     And the sweet heart sinks in its wounds,
     A gradual precipitation.

The Coming of the Grain

And spare your tears. For I am one
To whom the sun's each practice shone
Against the coming of the grain.

On my deathbed I shall repel
All courtesies. I'll make my will,
Through the drizzle of northern nightfall, call.

I'll leave the daylight to proud women:
Birdsong embroidered from collar to hem
To witty lads who sleep with them.

And the night like iodine
With its sharp purples, felt not seen,
To wounded and to desolate men.

I owe a debt to circumstance
Which in a woman was too kind once.
That debt is my son's inheritance.

Let me be poor. That debt will last
Till all the profit of her breast
Is paid in pain and pain is past.

I take upon me the heavy day
And, millstone-necked by what I see,
I grind all chaff, all straw away,

Undo life's delicate miracle
And let low organisms fall.
To me the part means more than the whole.

I *am* a part, and that's my function,
I'm not eternity's extreme unction,
And I must be taken in close conjunction

With whisky, females and income-tax laws,
Not with the final or primal cause.
I follow nothing but my own nose.

This is the hard beginning, here
And now, and high and dry, near
To nothing but beginning's fear;

Head and shoulders above the town,
Lonely, going against its grain,
Quietly, like a dying man.

Out of the house I look back now
Over whoever that man was who
Sat on the high stool filled with straw.

Far outdistancing metaphor
I fight without any commotion or stir
At table and chair behind the door,

Fight to make me an instrument
Of bright proportions, austere and bent
Upon nothing other than all men want.

The poetry is an incident
Forced upon men who take the hint
And say no more than what is meant.

The poetry must not matter now
When freedom is a circus show
Which only those on the tight-rope **know**.

Out of the belly love of brutes
A chaos chuckles and darkness shoots
Over the lanky scaffoldings' lights.

A million interruptions fall,
Each more little, each more still
Than a man climbing a climbing hill.

This is the night of terrible souls
Strayed from their branches, night that fulfils,
In panic's disorder, the tenderest kills.

And I under a lonely roof,
Look back, writing the calendar off,
Look back down the day as long as a life.

Look back among the blessed faces
Scattered together in books of addresses
And write wherever truth digresses.

Laid lowly there on the carpet where prayers
Bow down and ask for nothing, fear
Only promises and forgive despair.

I shall be better able then
To know what all these small things mean,
My seat of straw, the skeleton,

This monstrous pity for myself
And him, the meaning of the filth
We fight, and our proud duty's wealth.

Out of the level-headed ruin,
The burden of the afternoon,
Girls like choruses sung out of tune.

Out of it all, I now come back
Paid by the poor and healed by the sick,
I, the accusers, come back and speak.

Against the city's side-tracked wheels
The fools who rise, the blood that falls
With an artillery of vowels.

Upholster Hell and Heaven too.
Let them divide us when we're through.
Put me wherever he cannot follow.

Out of the coffin's wooden breast
To accident let him be cast
One with those labourers without rest.

Spare your tears. He is a man
For whom the sun to no purpose shone,
Who took the name of life in vain.

Let him continue it and spend
Eternity in his mankind.
At work in dung with pigs of the mind.

Or here explode him out of sight
Pump bullets through all those who fight
On the wrong side of the heart.

Let us be white blood that heals
While on a carpet of upright nails
The angel of the tramcar kneels.

Yellow and white are our only colours.
We are Samson robbed of his pillars.
We must be mad to kill our killers.

The aching sympathy of the flesh
Unwinds me towards him till I wish
I could allow our bodies to touch

Once in mutual forgiveness, once.
No! hush that word's extravagance!
There's no forgiveness for this dunce.

For then, he smiles . . . the boss . . . the big
Blue smile, a cold animal hug.
This is the hole those shadows dug.

My grave, and his grave too, the grave
Of all the world, and of love,
The grave that none will ever leave,

None will outlive. I feel the smile
Strutting and cold and pitiful
With its rank ceremonial.

All this is platitude and the small
Hot porcelain the crucible
Of song, exactly beautiful,

Is wept on, watered, trodden down.
We, the singers, are desperate men.
Our guns are forgeries. We burn

Our locks. They are our enemies.
The words we use are filled with spies
That turn the truth like milk to lies.

And to escape all this we run
Into extremities alone
'Amantio disposition on.'

The platitudes are everywhere
In speech itself, and poetry mere
Jargon of felons mouthing their hair.

[136]

Yes, we are Hamlet. Straw
Against the grain, unnatural, dry,
Salt carcasses within the sea.

Then at lunchtime stop and totter
Among the street fogs thick
Streets where even the wind seems to stutter.

But often in the tram I hear
Between the clattering stumble of years
Birdsong forcing entrance there.

Birdsong, that sharp embroidery
Of chirruping straw in the dovetailed sky
Or needling pollen pinned to a tree.

Then the world's an aqueduct
That catalytic metals tricked
Into the properties of luck.

The work gathers about my joy,
The birdsong like a battle cry
One way directs its scattered flow.

Then I return to rough and tumble,
The magazines' names with which I fumble,
The boss who butts in with gossip and grumble.

Out of the grunt and the tramcar's snort,
Stagger of signs and the motor's retort,
Glides the good angel high as a fort.

He passes and his steps repeat
Flower by flower, note by note:
Like a carpet through the street.

Power and pattern beyond law.
I, on my dry green stool of straw
Am crouched like a prayer for what I saw.

Then the corn, the new machines
That thresh it wonderfully fine,
All these return and each alone.

Shovels at ankles, picks at waists,
This daily congregation rests,
Made out of bones deformed with cysts.

Rests for a while where each one digs
Pitfalls to parcel whirligigs.
All are weary: none relax.

The grunt of horns, the sear of brakes,
Girls like tunes through humdrum blocks
Are audience. The guilt awakes.

To mend the disorder that dotes in my mind
He comes in the homely way of mankind
Smashing the wind's vase in his hand.

Then the daylight largely wasted,
Then the darkness never tasted
Joy the sorrow ill-digested:

Gurgle of straw in clotted stream,
Scanty skeleton's anger, shame
These in refrain beneath the dream.

These come back his voice to be
And fix attention heavily
Upon the loss within the lie.

Then the face's twisted pain
That once seemed happy in disdain,
Looks like vagrants, tracked down, moved on.

Then the canvas crammed with straw,
Mattressed bunks for men who die,
The grain ripped from them dry and raw.

Foreign words make heavy weather
And city streets chime at the end of their tether
A lovely community chancing together.

So that the place of my ink-stained desk
Is taken by storm to a straw-built nest
On the crest of a world just after the next.

But not for long though it is late.
Forever! For people come with their teeth white set
Into the smile against the heart,

Hurry their ways upon me, make
Small conversation mine. I take
My part and space diminishes back.

Come with cakes, small hours of talk,
Riot and righteousness and talk,
Talk until space diminishes back.

Into the street, the hallmark place
Of everything's slick use screen kiss
Where nothing could be better or worse.

Out of the street like a hunch-backed sailor,
Duck-gaited, badly in need of a tailor
Wobbles the fly-weight prophet and killer.

[139]

He stamps about like a Sunday tripper,
Posts his name on my blotting paper,
Bamboozles me, then butts in like a copper.

My high green stool is filled with dust,
With powdered straw I seem to taste
As I undo the parcels addressed

Some from the shop across the road,
Some from the ocean's other side,
All to the firm by which I'm paid.

Out of the packages' brown-paper names
Emerge a messenger footed on thumbs,
A voice that struggles like straw that swims

To take stock of the distant places
Scattered together in books of addresses
That are alive with people's faces.

He comes in the homely way of mankind
Post-marked through space and pigeon-brained
When space breaks out of its vase with the wind.

From Teneriffe to Maryhill,
Stark additions of names that fall,
Thornliebank to Aix-la-Chapelle.

Out of the sensual habit of truth
Daily the man comes discoursing with
Neither glib usage nor purpled mouth.

He is whatever man I meet:
I was no other: he is what
Happens to me each day I sit

In the quiet corner like
A small child riding a borrowed bike
Among the other people's books.

There is no end to him except
A token payment of our debt
With all of my life remaining yet.

Beginning the day I arrive late
And more of my apologies fit
The smile of excuse with which I am met

And the bright aftermath of sorrow
Not in an ounce the splendid universe
Will bail out cargoes or its tides reverse.

At the divide of compartments of rust:
Or those light-headed that trump up lust
In films, in football, the name of Christ.

Or poetry or politics, anything else
That is used to level the high-handed kills,
Presumptuous prayers or the drunk to the gills.

It's no use scolding the world. It's better,
Older than us, and maybe we clutter
Its broad-toned language with our stutter.

Look behind the curtain of prayer
With these wide eyes that open like doors
Into fulfilment everywhere.

Spare your tears. He is a man
For whom the sun's each practice shone
Against the coming of the grain.

And on his deathbed he repels
All courtesies. He makes his will;
Because I go against the grain.

Out of the happenings of truth
Without glib usage or purpled mouth
I come describing my daily youth.

The revelations have another place,
This is for office hours. I trace
The continual crisis of growing wise.

Perhaps a little pompous, ye
Years are as difficult a debt
To leave unpaid and we need to admit.

Beginning from the place I work
With magazines and such-like muck,
Scholarly rubbish heaped up dark

Round the intellects of men
Whose illuminations harden again
For the doom of death and the death of pain.

By nicotined lamplight and loggerheads
I go goodbying and meet instead
The jumbled traffic of homecoming bodies.

The high constructions of daylight dim,
Birdsong fades out, the girls don't hum
But are glad-eyed over with eyes like a thumb.

I have a debt to circumstance
For it was kind in a woman's glance.
The debt is my son's inheritance.

The lovely community chancing together
Where foreign names make heavy weather
And city streets shine at the end of their tether.

That's all I have but that will last
Till the whole profit of her breast
Is paid in pain and pain is past.

For me the part is more than the whole.
I *am* a part and that's my function.
I'm not eternity's extreme unction
And I must be taken in close conjunction.

Oracle Engraved on the Back of a Mirror

I

Syllogism of the solipsist as he was
Or had a name or hid to teach us that
We could believe in the incredible
And one of us

Standing at ease at last among downpouring
Ideologies and criss-crossed themes,
The sport of history, urine, blood and semen
Entering and restoring,

Shook down the notion that his shape had been
Fashioned from earlier when without surmise
Hot Permian sands dried Lycopodial jungles
And baked a bone

Till giant reptiles died of constipation
And progeny endowed with small hot blood
Got up on hind legs and digested grasses
And went to stud

To breed this syllogism here now who
Attends, attains, solipsist hypostatized,
The poise that these connected contradictions
Rejoice, renew.

Deduct that image and this knowledge is
Reduced below brain level: Leonardo
Could not see rocks except through the perspective
Of jellied eyes.

And so geology: the wet nerve tingles
With interruptions but the aforesaid plan
Is not gainsaid: instead synapses stutter
Out evolution's jingles.

Not in the rocks but in the nerves I'm made
Into a world of rock, of Permian sand:
The geologic aftermath will be dead
If I misunderstand.

We fail to find: we fail and then we fall.
There's no connection afterwards since we can't
Find anything to connect with: and only we
Are inescapable.

Yes. Joyce was right. We fail to follow what
Our ancestors, their words delimit thought,
Thought out across to us. We fail, then fall,
Misunderstanding all.

And Freud was right, and everyone is right:
We cannot be mistaken: each mistake
Is a discovery of the way we make
Our sins shine bright.

And yet we fail. We must find more mistakes
To make a language 'simple and sufficient'
For the immaculate wrongness of our lives:
The rocks need earthquakes.

Understand rightly, yes, I would do that.
But if I'm right I have not understood
The thing I suffer from, the sin I am
Always arriving at.

II

I understand the reptiles and the sand
But not my understanding: and I would rather
Have lived as always through these last few lines
Than have been thought an honest man.

For thought is always and only thought:
The thinking's different: thinking's in the blood,
The blood and sand and in the reptile's tail:
Therefore we fail

To find the thought that will express the thinking,
The language of the action, and the right
Action to express the everlastingness
Of what we fight.

Call it those nights those reptiles copulate
Incestually with ourselves, call up the sand bone,
Also my ancestor, call the desert wind
I consummate,

If they reverberate prophecies of the known
Ignorance I've been formulated as
In message to myself: through my discovery
I must atone

For the full majesty of my funeral deed
And for my birth within the great stone's seed,
For my humility presumption dread
Generosity greed.

Humble geology continually takes its place
Among the animal motions I perform
And takes the strain of one part of forever,
But it cannot grace

Itself with anything that isn't part
Of better brains than mine: and even mine
Knows all that's knowable and extends its knowledge
By breaking up my heart.

For to escape out of self-knowledge would
Not only kill what's knowable of me
But also end all knowing, mine alone
Being the knowledge of my good.

And yet I'm known by things I do not know.
I'm recognizable by what's not myself.
Still, I'm not contrary. I'm a lazy man
Bone-ready to agree.

I'll be red mercury or Permian sand
Well-oxidized, full of iron. Red. Red. Red.
I am reflecting just those things he said
And did not understand.

He was a syllogism and therefore was
Unprovable beyond the formal person
Who was the logic that he tried to prove
By such impersonal laws

As me and you and whom he might have been
If stones had not been bloody or the blood
Not mineral: but, as it was, himself
He fell between

The knowledge of his ignorance and his ignorance
Of the value of any knowledge: these contested
The right to teach him nothing but the sense
In which his premises could not be tested.

He reached the heavy cliché, being human,
Of discovering that the human person was
A formal barrier to the understanding
Of life's inhuman laws.

Analysis of an Archaic Ultimatum

Swift took it up, this business of false images,
Modest as always, on the ha'penny scale:
Milton, who bellowed against false marriages,
Never read Braille.

So John Adams, 'shy with awe and concern,'
Excised the lie from Constitutional Law,
To find he had invented it again
In Congressmen.

Now Wittgenstein; he bid us play the game
In the full knowledge that we shall be cheated.
They were all toys for every flame they played with,
Justly defeated.

Therefore we'll put the fires of Hell itself
Into an oven where we hope to cook
An entertainment for that 'little party'
Next on our book.

We, who are playthings, shall be players here,
Inventing rules, eliminating gambits,
While being pushed religiously like hand-outs
From square to square.

Ourselves the pieces that our lack of skill
Manoeuvres on a bill-board-plastered brain,
An economic trinket with a will
To show disdain.

The clay that used to represent our grave
Will be a quarry where we mine round marbles:
Buried in playthings, the tongue within the head
Bulges and burbles.

In the dark mouth where Chaucer's naked words
Copulated and gave birth its quality
Indolent mushrooms, verbal Christmas trees
Flicker with electricity.

We parcel words in tinsel like toy trains,
Toy trains of thought that clatter on tin rails
Trains with no timetable and no destination,
No passengers or freight.

And that's why Moses broke the Ten Command-
    ments:
Moses, who wrote on them, shattered the tables:
We keep our copies whole, inside a cupboard
Reserved for fables.

We have no Aaron: he and his
Golden calf are our hypothesis:
We are ourselves the golden cows
To whom we make our vows.

(Marriage at best, a social divinity
To usurp the direct inhuman contact:
From human limitations human beings contract
Intimate anonymity.)

Yes, each of us an image on his own,
Do it yourself and make your god at home:
Had we been there Moses might well have thrown
A second load of stone.

For again we have been lost, the falsehood of self-
     hood found:
An immodest man can't run to respect for his enemy
Though he can't even fight except in imitation
Of his enemy's reputation.

But God, our enemy, necessarily unseen,
Excludes such combat by fighting without
Fear or the wish to injure
Us by his censure.

Though we've given Him the shrapnel, yet He
     doesn't blow Hell
Out of the bits of us that aren't there:
He tries to let us see to it that He could do as
     well
If, as we aren't, He wasn't aware.

We never fight Him; but just because we can't
Escape ourselves to find a battlefield.
We can only pretend, and we always do, of course,
That we've got what we want.

It's still expedient to pretend we have
Somebody else's love.
Expediency is a notion with its nerve
Screwed to a normal curve.

It's expedient to pretend we don't feel pain.
(Expediency itself is the total pretension.)
When we come to our death-beds, then we pretend
Incomprehension.

For suffering must be stopped.
We're humans of the humanist persuasion.
The intellect is a neurotic lesion.
Offending nerve-fibres must be chopped.

Physical suffering's even more easy
So long as there are nurses who don't get queasy
When their unconscious patients are needle fed
With liquid bread.

Suffering, indeed, is quite inhuman.
It may even, ultimately, be divine;
In which case no sensible man or woman
Will allow it to go on.

Aaron's golden baby cow
Could probably advise us how
Best to endure pain and the ache
Of a changed shape.

Though she was melted in a pot
And poured sweating into a mould
I doubt if she felt over hot
Or, later, too cold.

Expediency creates the painless false image,
As Swift pointed out in the case of George the First.
After resultant debasement, even the simplest values
Cannot be re-imbursed.

And expediency is the opposite of responsible de-
    cision:
Riveted lecherous corpses, Milton thought them,
Bedded and buried in an archaic ceremony,
Barred from deciding the one thing on which they agree.

But, above all, expediency negatives Law,
The impersonal experience of contrary expedients:
The possibility that there might be a human integrity,
A correct obedience.

The probity of poetry may be by-passed.
The expedient gamesman can't play fair.
The expedient farmer will probably be the last;
And strontium pollutes the air.

But what must not, the objective imagination,
Rediscovering unceasingly in a different generation
The Law within the Law, that reads the Law,
Like Adams, with awe.

Yet now our Law books like the other toys
Are heaped in comfortable libraries
Where false men study the false images
Cast by their eyes.

No shyness now, another sphere of knowledge
To be absorbed in an appropriate college.
Even the seminary for theology
Makes no apology.

For, knowing everything, or how to learn
The way to learn it; we worship what we know
And promise that we'll master what we don't
Yet quite discern.

We worship inwardly our knowledge of
What's still beyond conception and
Don't let our ignorance get beyond
Our power to prove.

Aaron's golden baby cow
Was something somewhere anyhow.
What we worship's just the rate
We worship at.

Each man a mirror for each other's mind
Is worshipped at the same time as defined.
Each man alone thinks himself unforeseen
And won't come clean.

He wants to keep a secret from statistics,
A little hovel full of light and sweetness
Where he can contemplate and conjure greatness
Just like the mystics.

Each, a false image, worships a false image
Of the false images that worship him.
We hide behind the visibility
Of what we see.

Thus we get Moses and the Ten Commandments,
Obeyed by some and worshipped by the others.
(The disobedient to Leviticus mutter
That we're all brothers.)

And therefore Moses breaks his Ten Commandments.
Moses, who wrote on them, shatters the tables.
The Word of God escaped the Israelite
Through words from God.

He, breaking laws, replaces testaments
By something that we can't reduce to fables.
Moses, unjustifiably right,
Negates his fraud.

Dry sticks don't blossom when his anger breaks
His Covenant. He doesn't give us back
An image like the image of the cow
He powders down.

He bears another witness altogether.
He vouches with a puddle of dry sand
For the untruth of what we thought denoted
By what we quoted.

It legislates where it lies, raped
By the solar imagination's intrinsic thunder:
Splintered beneath Moses' anger, the Law
Explodes into shape.

He gives us an image for what we cannot imagine.
An alphabet stutters to reach the articulate brain.
But the shape that is shaped by its letters is dust,
Dust and some stone.

Ground Plan for a Church

Façades come later. The designer uses
The first rib that Adam ever had
And carves it with exactly the same instrument
As once carved chaos.

To keep at it, to keep at it, that's the trick;
To forget about crockets, bosses, quadripartite vaults,
Limiting delineation to nave, choir and transepts
And simple arithmetic.

To keep infinity out and the exciting gradients
Elevations presume when they're not measured in
Terms of underlying ditches, ruts if you like,
The human medians.

A church is built to contain people,
A population container: and yet it is meant to be
One place at one time,
Time's staple.

You too are aware that every man lives
In a different place from every other
And is surrounded by different patterns of time,
Disparate ogives,

And that a coincidence in the desultory
Movement of legs and backsides can never
Range two men side by side
In the consistory.

[156]

So it becomes necessary to devise a space
That will condense their movements to one time only
Not conflicting areas of experience, no, not above all
The human race.

The species is definable, zoologically delimited
And reasonably distinct:
But the reason itself arranges the very partitions
That must be assimilated.

The reason itself is an historical asset
Conditioned by its own transcriptions of the evidence.
This church must be built of a sort of stone that will
  contradict history
Or, better, by-pass it.

Old stones, if they are hard, are best for this. They
  have
Brought their origin forward to the point where
Change is unlikely, so that their history
Must behave.

And ground too should be carefully chosen
So that it is always pitched plumb centre on the
  horizon
Where sunset and sundown, for different men,
Mix in one orison.

Each shrug of the earth must be synchronised
At the level of the foundations.
But there must be no Euclidean lines on the drawing
  board,
Nothing idealised.

Each detail matured slowly like good wine,
An immediate exactitude in the general proportions,
Numerals as part of the aesthetic evidence, all drawn
Into complete design.

For this house is meant as man's guest house for
 God
As creation is God's for man.
It is needed because the human animal cannot
Be understood

Except, perhaps, when a long reconciliation
Between him and his God is broken by
Immediate quotidian proximity
And the resultant retaliation

Of God through the knowledge of sin that His
 presence brings
Against sins forever forgotten:
So that man knows the sin of his knowledge and
 sings
In praise and terror of such things.

It is necessary, therefore, that the building should not
 interpret.
It should simply be of such dimensions as will contain
Men
And God should be able to sleep quietly in the transept.

Perhaps, after all, the Mosaic Tabernacle,
Its nomadic agility substantiating an ubiquitous God,
Brought time to a standstill and, since then,
All has been architect's prattle.

Certainly the Heavenly Examiners
Have given few signs of being satisfied by
The various foundations laid down by our designers
And raised to the sky.

Perhaps, of course, we have been too modest.
Perhaps we have not believed with enough fervour
That, however badly our building was conceived,
It was still our best.

We laid our plans too low.
We did not understand
That everything we do
Is always true.

In the end our church cannot stand too high.
Once drawn, the thin boundaries may be steepled
Up to whatever pinnacles our engineers can warrant
As strict possibility.

Invocation of Fact

Facts, as intelligence understands so well,
Are propositional facts of experience;
Facts, as my demons know, as angels tell,
Sometimes lead to Hell.

That's neither here nor there. It's certainly not here
Since I'm here. (Or am I a fact?)
I fill the space. But when I'm filled with beer
I disappear.

Or maybe I am it, the fact at large
Among the anxious angels? Maybe I know myself?
Or the beer knows me? It's certainly inside,
A fluid charge.

Too much is certain and too fluidly.
I half believe that you are you are me.
But I can't recognise; and even as I try
Dead people die.

The flight of ghosts, always mysterious
And always commonplace and always on,
Abrupts my measures. I'll have nothing else
To say till dawn.

Yes. I am frightened. But I'm still the same
And neither the great dreadful facts like ants
Nor dreams however simple ever came
Up to my grasp.

The octopus within the wedding ring
Has loved me well, begetting squeaking children.
But there's a fact that makes the marriage sing
And the bells ring.

Or is there? That's the question. Or? Or else?
Perhaps there are a hundred thousand girls
And more for copulation—and none rebels
That's what the truth foretells.

But Lesbians forbid a man come near?
But are they women? Are there men who fear
The rejection of a sexual deaf-mute
That they can't hear?

Yes, there are some. We must stick to the facts,
Since truth must be extracted like a tooth
And every proposition just attracts
Another artifact.

If facts won't hold nothing else will
That's a good argument. But if facts won't, what
Will hold us steady till our heads distil
Facts from our thoughts.

Perhaps we do know better. Even, perhaps,
We could be better, though I doubt it, but
Perhaps we could be better, and that traps
Us into another lapse.

We will not, can not, do not, never admit
That we are made of the same stuff as shit,
And yet we know we are, and that's just it
And that's why we must quit.

We can't contend with gods. We're propositions
Pulverised by the smallness of our lives.
We are the learners of the new positions,
But we can't bear transitions.

Yes, we are perfect facts. We don't
Believe in what we are, but we're still ready
To support the guilty or the innocent
If they are so already.

Description of Why

I might, of course, by getting killed, inscribe
My name invisibly on one. I can even,
With priggish devotion, imagine my dying
For what I believe in.

I'm certainly not against killing. Vindictive
And normally knowing, I follow my enemies
With hatred secreted as organically as
A snake's venom is.

In secret session, plenary selves resolve
On items that their minutes must refute.
The powers-that-be are just the powers that they
Would execute.

Therefore, in secret session, in small conclave,
Murder's dismissed while the death-warrant's
    written.
One man, however sub-divided, can't
Become Great Britain.

My handshake isn't lethal and my smile
Lacks the temper of a spry stiletto:
I can't employ the labour, buy the bricks
To build a ghetto.

But, if I could, its slums would gurgle with
A hideous excess of chums and cronies,
And intellectual filibustering blues
From sexual phoneys.

The noise of questions would be stopped by groans.
And costumes in their giggling colours would
Fester to grey rags. The garbage cans
Would market food.

And if, by chance, some delegates to my
Congress of selves suggested a revision,
They'd find the others anxious to agree
To ego fission.

And find themselves inside. Reply. Reply.
Across that barrier voices spill the word
That stainless must mean silent and no echo
Of tears is heard.

All man-mosquitoes must be swotted down,
Their bloodstreams poisoned, so that when they've
    fed
As usual on each other, two by two
Will leave four dead.

While, across, within the stainless city
My funeral persons would convene committees.

Sparks are Splendid

Try the impossible and then stand back.
You'll see the ancient verities explode.
That 'love your neighbour' lark goes up in smoke
And 'God is love' sparks and the sparks are splendid.

Someone complains, 'This isn't what I meant,'
But someone's no one since you have decided
That the impossible is what you want
And not a place in anybody's bed.

Cows which are fertilised by serpents know
Just what you need, and their horns are a goad.
You must adventure on the path they trod,
Encumbered now by every kind of load.

And on the way you'll find as you pass by
Adventurers return discomfited.
Their beaten feet will talk to you and say,
'We stink because our master was derided.'

And you press on. Fireworks illumine your
Part of the path to nowhere, never mended.
You see the flaws and, seeing them, begin
To listen to the distance of the road.

A Diseased Truth

What happens to a diseased truth?
Does it creep under the collar bone
And enter the lung
So that words spoken are rancid?

Is it crushed and distorted further
By thought after glittering thought?
Does it hibernate in the brain
Where the tired systems converge?

Does it copulate with a lie
And beget history?
Is it a good mixer?
Or does it sit silent at parties?

And what relationship can it have
With a truth that is whole and full?
Does the contagion spread
At their very first contact?

Or can the truth heal the disease
With the bold calm hands of a surgeon?
All these things have happened and will.
There are many diseases of truth.

Respect

Maybe in China's communistic village,
Too small for bombs and far too poor for pillage,
Where drunken poets squander through the night
And lazy economics turn out right,
Maybe in China human intellect
Will recognize an object with respect.

Here there is nothing. Recognition spills
Over a surly testament of wills

The shape in shallows in my mother's anguish
Upturns a tousled boy beneath my language
And puts his Sunday pinafores on top
Of this huge nakedness through which I drop
The shape in shallows, the reflecting shape,
Takes all the sheer disaster and escape.

How long ago and in my hand and nearer
Are these things now, exterior endearer
Of my own childhood keeping track of each
Stray loosening, the film of baby speech!
How long ago you make it since today
I will not question with my roundelay

Among such prodigies of gratitude,

And am betrayed from litany to lilac,
Forced octaves upwards to confound a skylark,
To dance, a lost man, on a heap of heights
Where musics gravitate like satellites,
And are betrayed down corridors of milk
Dizzy leviathan in chains of silk.

O my far fallen, fetched from a wretched resting,
The red and round-voiced berries lit for nesting
Persuade a daisy's discipline to bend
Where my own knees like trees . . . and trees . . .
   extend.
And my far fallen, fetched too high, endure
Their lost humility and final cure.

How can the loud-mouthed burly hint that hallow?
That dowels nebulae with pegs of tallow?
Or ties a crocus into the tongue of Spring,
Half uttered and unheard, then hears it sing?
How can the loud and wilful world give thanks
For what it is and knows not, coins and clanks?

April's blithe watchword through a throat of trees
In pursed semantics in the city's footsteps
Challenged the outside forward shouting 'Friend.'

Words

Rotting the tongue, the words go fumbling on,
Plain words and trellissed encumbrances
To every communication.
Somewhere between them, a truth dances.

Rotting the ear, the words keep coming, coming
Through straight ways or by devious circulation
Emerging from behind.
A gimlet truth goes out ahead of them.

Rotting the eyes, the tears keep falling, falling
Down all the wrinkles grief has already made
Upon the sunburnt face.
Its flesh remains. Death's stalwart grin is hidden.

Rotting the fingers that with their rotten tips
Can feel only myself
Rebounding from the world
Sensations plentifully speak of health.

But on the tongue is the wrong word. The ear
Listens to itself. The eyes are drained.
The fingers falter, cannot keep their grip:
I have allowed myself to be explained.

The Limits of Movement

I mark my limits on an alighting whirl
      Of wings near daybreak
Birds that are fetch into the sunlight call
      Me by mistake.
I hear the sun that bars my path unfurl
      Songs in my wake.
It keeps me and, in its gallant mood, it will
      Rise for my sake.

We climb down into the street. The smoke
That took my breath away, you took
From such a dot of light. And O,
My dear, as we both turn to go
Back to the herring town where pubs
Await their crews from little ships,
The light and blindness disappear
Together—these songs grow all the more clear.

What a pale text I have put on.
But who is there here who can fathom
This brazen town suddenly quiet
—Not even milk yet laid out?
All else we know to be beyond
Us now. Confined here we both wonder
Whether, like these stones, we must also
Be quarried, built with, before we can grow.

Roll up. Roll up. See the stage-cut stars on the
    streets
Every performance is a first-night showing.
Every entrance the last—and there are no exits.

A Small Grief has been Launched

These headlands clench their bare grey talons
Deep into the splash of water, and they scrape
Whitenesses out of waves caught half off-balance
By the burly steadiness of this gaunt cape.

And further out, invisibly exiled there,
Where the full swim of the sea floats salt shoals
Over its bows, under its keel, there rolls
That one small grief, that broken part of prayer.

Of course unseen, naturally, because
The scream of rocks scraping the edge is me.
I am deserted for those anonymous
Regularities of the implacable sea.

Though I can't follow it, though I must
Grasp scant purity from the shallows; although
These stones, my selves, this humid solid dust
That baulks the ocean determines all I know.

There is the grief in exile; somewhere, it
Divides distance, punctuates freedom, soars.
I stand and grasp at water, squat, spit,
Myself my anchor since my selves are shores.

But still the grief, no longer mine, makes free
With every weather and sails on out,
Safe agent, slackened by no rusting doubt
Since it obeys each inch of each decree.

Bound to that wave, it bounds away to this:
Missing, it topples: toppling, is rescued by
The waters of its previous jeopardy:
Directions take it now, a dot of distance.

A dot of distance keeping to its course
Away from me, it rides those changing laws,
This little grief, once mine, now lost in hoarse
Commands that carry it: and yet it draws

The best of me and what I hope to learn
Out into depths these talons cannot reach
And over depths unknown to any speech
Towards shores that dwarf my blind but best concern.

A Sort of Language

Who, when night nears, would answer for the
  patterns
Words will take on? emerging huge, far, shiny,
What unfrequented systems? Or like clouds
Unseen and hiding brightness, bringing rain,
Progressions that the wind drives on, drives after,
Who will say? I who have seen, seen many,
Imagining I scattered them abroad,
Starlight for Calvary and the immense equations
That drew to unity two who know not either,
As to a hill at midnight, I have seen words,
Seen them with thanks too, shivering, become
Fragile and useless, pale as the steel sparks
Tramcars make waifs of when they round a corner.

Without a Thought

I have been there. I have been back
Like rabbits on the selfsame track
Sniffing eternity. I've been
        Unheard, unseen,
Unmannered and unknown as any man
        Can ever half become
If half remains the same.

And having sniffed the greatness out
Of many things and with much thought
Respired delight, I've come to this
        Conclusion, finish,
That all the things I ever have loved kiss,
        Blow bloom and blossom rot,
        And love without a thought.

Greatness becomes this little clearer
Simplicity comes that much nearer
Because as I grow older I forget
        Just what I'm at,
And all the things that I've not met as yet
        Grow older with me and
        Give up or understand.

Greatness and nearness are not near
You must walk over, you must come here.
Come into my hand and let me show
        Yourself to you
And you, yourself, afraid though you are, to me.
        Greatness meets your fear
        You see it disappear.

Calamity makes much of us
For once we're not anonymous
People can talk. And still they can't
            Stop talking out
They like to talk. We'll not forbid their bent,
        We know that we will die.
        We'll reach ourselves that high.

The Best of It

The best of it is that I am at least
Made less by what is greater, and that I can't,
Reached by these words now, measure what's
    increased.

Your words make hay of me, but I'm released
By them from standing shivering and distant.
The best of it is that I am at least.

Knees soaked rheumatic by the promised harvest
You razed with scythe and sickle what I meant:
Reached by these words now, measure what's
    increased.

But you, like a horizon or a priest,
Past every boundary of the round land, went:
The best of it is that I am at least
Reached by these words now measuring what's
    increased.

The Terrible Stranger

He comes in hobnails right among the garden,
And his sheep bleat, the muck begins to harden
In stucco patches, filthy claws of wool,
Stained as the linen girls' frocks at school.
He comes in hobnails and does not taste the fruits
That overhang the droppings of his brutes.

He has the harvest, he the terrible stranger,
Made from the moon's face, in a horsey manger,
He hacks at roots, picks back the winning seeds,
And havocs the ripe life that in them bleeds.
He has the harvest, this bitter, hair-brained
Man in the moon's mountains, as he's disdained.

Speak to him slowly and he rounds an answer
With intricate precision like a dancer.
Don't over-emphasize or start to cry.
He has endured much and he did not die.
Speak to him slowly and make no mistake
He is most honest when his words most ache.

My Song

This countryside rises beside my song
Because my song is the same as that old one
Silent perhaps then but by the sap in the first
Gymnosperms near here sung to the tune of the sun,
And sung on the ocean's surface when plankton
    outburst
I do not know how many years ago
And today again, and tomorrow, rising along
All paths incessantly, and rising to
The tops of trees, and mountain tops, my song
Whose essence is probably magic, and certainly
    peaceful.

The essence is probably magic, is certainly peaceful
Compared to machinery's intonations outside,
The rapid flicks clocks turn up like tea-leaves
Written, re-written, corrected and unapplied,
On future worlds no present world believes;
The churn of the concrete-mixer, an engine that
    throbs
In disappearing whispers out of the town:
And davits and furnaces, needles and pincers and
    knobs
Creeping with power, the power that lets us down,
While my song quietly searches for emphasis.

Yes, my song quietly searches to emphasise
An older and more capable force: that
Which begun, and in the beginning began; force
Gracious and gradual, incitement into what

The pedigreed instants feel for and find in the course
Of a century's silence, living within them and sing:
As though an anvil taking what white steel
Most wishes shape to be, makes steel ring
Not with a dead sound but a victorious peal
And as that steel would sound let my song be.

Now as that steel would sound, let my song be
Carried across the hilltops and then subside
Into the villages and in the towns
That keep my country close to the sea's side
Let it be heard, for I have found what once
Seemed an impossible gesture of the mind,
Projection of a crypt filled with imaginary
Saints of a nimble and unearthly kind
Who held my heart in safe repository
And to these ghosts my every song was sung.

Home Thoughts from Home

I was beginning somewhere in Manhattan,
Was pre-arranged with cubicles of satin,
The scissors sterilised, the womb in screams,
When someone dipped me in a pot of dreams,
Was just beginning heaven in my head
When they transmuted its mad mint to lead.

That's how it happened. Then the cradle curdled.
What obstacles were left there ghosts have hurdled,
The dregs of night, bedclothes, the tousled sun,
Cleared by the crabs by whom man's race is run.
That's how it happens. Now I sit and think
Until I am the liquor that I drink.

I am none other than Villon in prison,
I meet Confucius with rhymed derision
And stick my tongue out at the gods of Baal.
I am the wire that blinds the nightingale.
I am none other than the Athenian lord
Who rapes the church because his friends are bored.

Or all gone down—a bomb in 1940—
A murdered tenement. They call me 'Shorty'
As beggarly I squat on that same place
With shrapnelled joists and walls that bare no trace.
All, all gone down, or gone away in grit.
A fly's eye pivoted and noted it.

That's just like me—the fly I mean—the lenses,
Though I'm the maximum that time dispenses,

To see it happen and not do a thing.
I am fed up with all these ghosts that sing.
It's just like me to sit here after all
And wait for an immortal doom to fall.

Paper and table, then to bedtime later.
Nothing gets done and I am its narrator.
I trounce the milky systems which require
This death by ash, experiment by fire,
Paper and table and the clock goes round,
Round like twin dice, but round, and round, and
    round.

For this place daily pranks a new procession.
Let Winter be a hypnotist's expression,
Then Spring pops out canary eyes and tries
The juggler Summer's gay complexities.
Yes, this place daily—let the windows gape—
Autumn's sharpshooters falter—birds escape.

But not the heart, not agile as a swallow,
—A train of reasons—what has passed will follow,
An echo startling upwards for aloud
Webs the meridian to blood a shroud,
But not the heart can turn back one bad beat
To water a new world beneath its feet.

Maybe when China's communistic village
Learns that our poverty's too poor for pillage,
When drunken poets squander through the night
And lazy economics turn out right,
Maybe in China, human intellect
Will recognise an object with respect.

But no, not these men! Write to the newspapers.
Jest at deformities. An ulcer capers.
Have print marks on you like performing fleas
That piggy back and leapfrog and disease.
No, not with them men. Let the secret sore
Be opened up and sold from door to door.

I am a craftsman of medicinal plaster.
What will I bandage? There are no disasters.
These agate ironies I decorate
Tell me that time can never be too late.
I am a craftsman, and the honeycomb
Of centuries in anguish is my loom.

Tell me tomorrow if the day is shorter
By one bad dream. I am the proper quarter.
This crab-backed steeplechase is my affair.
Did you cut time? Come on now. Don't just stare.
Tell me tomorrow, sometime, not today,
And, if you kill time, throw the corpse away.

You've heard the radio, the highest mammal,
Fish the sound waves with tenterhook and trammel.
O what was that? A baby in a well
Screams for a coffin and the snows of Hell?
You've heard the radio and now I'll try
To beat back time by this apostasy.

I here resolve against the run of reason
To enter maytime for a winter season,
To turn the tables and the floorboards too
Until the clouds match bedrooms and are blue.
I here resolve to fish the graveyard dry
Of men I never met, with whom I die.

You, there, my father, brass tacks were your passion.
Your son is otherwise and out of fashion.
His algebraic amorals are thrown
Like bridges up towards nearer one unknown.
You there, my father, tell me, do you know
Can dice endure an everlasting throw?

Here, as I question, emptiness comes creeping
Backwards again. It is the old heart leaping,
Leaps back one beat, pelagic dinosaur
Or evil-eyed crustacean of the shore.
And as I question answers creep again
Over the hurdles of a baby's brain.

The prophecies run bridal riot hither.
Among my ghostly origins that dither
On plaster pinnacles a wounded man
Who cannot finish what the ghosts began,
The prophecies one patented and placed
On every sidewalk in the best of taste.

Home from the Sea

The longest days are those spent at sea.
Waves dip heavily, trundling under our gunwale
An imagination or promise of the ocean as abyss.
The longest days are those we can hardly remember.
Dead waters retire. The smoke lingers unshaven
Or lounges from cabins into a corridor where
It collides helplessly with the stink of coffee.

There is no steadiness anywhere except in the arrival
Of another wave or another morning. The same
Unsteadiness, waves morning by morning,
Jolts without jest our neurotic banter.

Slowly around us the air circulates like
A paper that everyone has already re-read
And will re-read later. Ghostly
The engines clamber through the floor.

Cards collect grease from many fingers. Dust
Rubs along the ward-room to the galley.
The great sea collapses harmlessly outside
An unopening door.

Slipshod and sleepy, we calculate who we are.

We sit beside the clock that thuds so softly
Around in circles and dictates our duties.
Its monosyllables never threaten us.
We know we're safe; since, though the ocean flexes
Its watery muscles with a vast display,

There is inside those ships which sail the farthest
A shabby but invulnerable place that hedges
Stability with repetitive concision.

The clock, in monosyllables, repeats,
Time out of mind and out of time with ours,
A mile, a mile, another mile, until
One day it stops, neglected, unwound,
The current turned off: this is our destination.

Corner Boy's Farewell

In the yellow room among the grey furniture I sit
  sorrowfully
Already sour with the wisdom of age and bitterly
  complaining.
Outside the evening sulks away.
The garden vegetation curls up like a cat.
The hillside tumbles a snug green wall.
Why do they keep coming back, the days we have
  spent together?
They come in their long lines but dancing and deep
  in the sun,
Deep in the sun, black and engraved in shadows.
Why do they keep coming back with such regular
  purpose?

First in the club-room,
The grumbling inconsequent people
Arguing art over stale tea-bread . . .
And I very young was greatly impressed.
You hardly saw me through their foggy heads.
Bluebottles clung to the damp flycatcher. My eyes
  were glued on your face.
You hardly saw me. Then you went away.

Between parting and our second meeting
Months passed and many things happened.
During that time my heart and mind were hid.

The twins of the wood were hid from woodcutters'
Eyes, from the temptations of the house of sugar.
I hid them alive in the shape of a drunken bout.
I put them to sleep in the dugs of a dried-up whore.
I silvered round in tinfoil cartons, talked them into the
    noisy drugs,
To hide from my grand accusers, from the huge
    scenery of your great disciples.
And yet when we finally met again,
You, half mad with your own problems:
I, an absconded schoolboy:
Our laughter was green in the London pubs
And a sympathy somehow occurred that was not to be
    laughed at.

And after that time the occasions of meeting gather:
From the ends of this country, from the cramped
    edges of experience
They trek in a single direction that makes us separate
    ever.
I cannot quite remember all the dates and places
But we have stood at corners, sat together
Between apprisal and dismissal,
Arrival and departure,
Between anticipation and delight,
Boisterous days and the long memory.
We have stood at corners and waited together.
What I remember best is saying goodbye
For that is most in the nature of friendship.

A week ago in this selfsame city
We said farewell and did not know we said it.
And I was left to revile in this rainy place.
O my poems, be against this city:

Its people badly dressed and without good manners,
The simplest necessities of life made lewd and
    tortuous.
Let them be things of a day.
Let my poems have bees' blood in them,
Let them be sharp but sensitive to honey.
For I still think of life as once of mist in Cornwall
Man-high and from the sea subsiding gently
Over the ploughed fields, brown, with scarce green
    growth,
But hidden under field-grey all that day,
Woven to one opacity.
Then on my eyesight the slant light broke
Of a single mist-drop narrowly slung to a cobweb
And each, the mist, through which my senses
    travelled
Broke at that sun-reflecting signal to its own:
The watered air grew bright with single claws:
So on the fine web spun from something stronger
One man can hold, precarious, complete
His own self's light that never is repeated
But acts as orrery to all the lights of others:
And that same web grows finer with its function,
More beautiful to praise with each drop held
In that peculiar tension once forever.

That's how I think of you and your calm discourse,
And thinking too the knowledge of a minute,
Planet's discovery or the seed of tree,
A new tree in a new place, something
To come, to grow gradually actual,
Thinking of this and that and all together
You grow so bright I sometimes seem to see
Walking between you and the direct sun

My evening-shadow struggling like a breeze
Until it climbs against it, smothers light
And drowns the sun out down beneath your face.

For that is the special human knowledge,
Knowledge of genesis
Of a brightness other than that of the day sun,
Outstaring and outstripping.
And this is human too
—Though valid more than for humanity,
Humanity its instrument—this knowledge
That I have hit on since you went
Of going further out than light can follow, rooted
    and separate,
Into America, my mind or sea.
This I prepare for and communicate
In the anticipation of my lifelong voyage
Of seeing what has always been most loved grow dim
    and disappear
Into perfection's prodigies of peace.

Into the sacrifice bitterly endless of all that man
    means
In terms of bones, breath, skin and brain,
Of his achievements, even the love humility
    achieved.
Love he can only like a beggar take
From the kind hand of passage hidden in his heart,
The hand that could be merciless as he,
Deny as he denies.

Love he is given, he who, like a beggar,
Squats where the virtues congregate their outpour,
He who is hasty when a dime of knowledge

Drops in his cap
To run and spend it in the nearest brothel
And then come howling back to the mercy and
   lucky downpouring.
This knowledge then of leaving all behind
All, that by wailing meanly, may attend my vigil.

Self-Portrait

Dedicated admittedly but still not knowing quite
By what book he had sworn what cause to defend.
With his last breath he assured us it would all turn
Out right.

A vague preference, always, for the other side of the
    case,
He staked his claim to the windows across the river.
And studied himself through a golden lattice,
    himself
In paraphrase.

He thought crime a good thing, criminals a bore:
He would willingly have murdered anyone worth
    killing
But his situation simply demanded that he should
Ask for more.

And he agreed that warmongers were entitled to
    make
Enough money to cover insurance on whatever lives
    they lost:
Anyone who denied this seemed to him to have
    missed
The force of their mistake.

The pulchritude of Mr Auden was
Something stammered after, stammered sometimes
But really when the bit came to the bit he found it
Comatose.

And so he bought from the second-hand dealers
A poetry that he didn't think much good.
It's said he joined a club for poetesses
But, perhaps, that's rude.

The Guy

He puts new clothes upon the man he borrows
To give an identity
To the victims who must suffer his false sorrows
And laugh and cry and die

As though they were himself. But he alone
In borrowed togs disguised
Trots past the sentries and his heart of stone
Is grim and unsurprised

By the loud massacres his name has searched
Throughout reality
And he avoided neatly, limped or lurched
Away from tidily.

His drunken stumbling had an aesthete's slant,
His mad ways method, and
If anyone had asked him what he meant
He'd fail to understand.

To juggle with gigantic puzzles,
To balance love on scorn
(Love that is bright and slippery and born,
Scorn that the big pig guzzles).

To keep the equilibrium of man
And heaven and hell in spate,
(A little envy there, a jolt of hate,
—But charity has won.)

[193]

To award prizes for the best kinds of pair
To justify sorrows
To put new clothes upon the man he borrows
And do it again and again,

A new turn-out for every old lout, Guy Fawkes,
And each in his turn burnt
In a bonfire made sacred by life's undercurrent.

Community of Worship

I believe in God.
It is not your God
Any more than it is my God.
It is not a member of the committees
That reflect international issues
While they perjure themselves with decisions.
It is not even
What goes on between us.
It is not
Kindness to the poor.
All these things are sometimes appropriate
(Even I am sometimes appropriate
And my god is not me.)
There are occasions—and you know them better than
  I do—
When loneliness is all that there is
And more than enough of it
Is enough.
There are dreams to which there is no admittance
—We all dream them.
There is a time which is secret,
Though only for us since the secret is
That there never was a secret between us.
But there is nothing
So difficult or so complete,
So hidden or so open,
So meaningless or so much the basis of meaning,
As the God we must both worship
Because there is no other.

Adam and Eve

He would do anything for her humblest sake,
That man of many talents, wisdom, strength.
And she, no shrew, permitted tenderly
His kisses to revere her mouth by mouth.

And so they passed each shorter afternoon
And each still shorter night as though they were
Both sons of God who very graciously
Had each been made the sole inheritor.

Meantime the world grumbled on outside.
The kings were killed and the small cities fell.
The wireless buzzed with rumours and some
    thousands
Claimed to have found the quickest route to Hell.

But he and she impassively continued
Their clinging roundabout, and children came
Who cried and coughed and called for more attention
Than could be given to them, each the same.

They were his followers, and her little dog
Led them across the frontiers toting pistols.
His laws were theirs, his judgments—of an apple,
His thoughts, his works, his poems—laundry lists.

The Naked Bankrupt Prince

His ermine swaddlings the cold of snow,
Black night for purple, the high desert
And sheep nuzzling, bleating low,
A camel-hair cloak wrapped round their shepherd,
A star, just one, four men from the east;
The legend has lost its trappings since
Renan's bastard and Yeats's beast
Unclothed the naked bankrupt Prince.

The Autumn Death

That Autumn Death was talking in the garden
—Not for the first time—but when Spring came
   round
It didn't stop. Instead, its quiet voice
Kept whispering nothings from the budding ground.

And so, he left the place. At first to Brighton
And drinks and dames and lobsters cooked in wine.
But the sea spat at him. The damp skies glowed
With memories that he took for a sign.

He ran again and reached the south of Spain
In time for almond blossom. Those white flowers
Studded the leafless trees with purity
That drained all pity from the truth it powers.

The woman who possessed him turned to stone.
The olives wrote their stunted message out
Against the sky. The fishermen brought up
Small lean clean things. He hardly dared to doubt.

When he came back he listened. Death was talking
In that soft voice he knew, talking to him.
He answered back and heard the echo calling
Death's name across the garden, suddenly trim.

Requiescat

I who have done enough
Have been undone three ways,
Now call my sickness off
With these obituaries.

I think that I died once
Out of pure innocence,
Once by the act, and once
By my quick human conscience.

And now these deaths are my
Imperishable pain,
So that I long to die
Again—just once again.

To Marie

For Half a Year of Happiness

November 6th: 1956

For half a year of happiness
　　Between us two
These small barefooted words must run
　　Along my pen to you.

They whisper secretly in one
　　Another's secret ear:
Heavy black-booted thoughts patrol,
　　But cannot hear.

This mob of children from the streets
　　Where love is young and we
Playing pavement games, chalk clumsy signs
　　And riddle-ree.

O do not be deceived, my dear.
　　Sing me a song.
These little gangs, in secret gay,
　　Have beaten down those long

Vocabularies, squads of words,
　　In sulky navy-blue.
There's half a year of happiness
　　Between us two.

Wife

She, she herself, and only she
Shone through her body visibly.

                                    Coleridge.

Your dark body deepens suddenly.
Over the meagre firth where children throw
Pennies for luck or where the drowned imago
Is eaten by orphaned infants, about as high
As the horizon's level in the eye,
An eager trapdoor swings upon a screw.
Already, as the door gives under you,
Its prodigies, secretly seen, uncover the lie
Of your deepening understanding, your
Motion towards palpable invisibility.
As usual, when things matter, some of us die.
I drown in what I am, among the obscure
Instants that cannot teach me to endure
Your dark body deepening gradually.

Gold

'Gold', I had always thought it an ugly poetic word
Swamped under associations and well past drowning,
Well past the point where corpses begin to stink.

But now I don't.
You are not fawn, not beige, not brown:
None of the prose words describe your colour.
You have the same tint as an old gold wedding ring.
A new word has been launched into language.

Goodnight

Lie on my left side, darling. It is time
For us to sleep now. Underneath us tumble
Keen little eyes like pincers which take aim
At the sad centre these delights preamble.
No, yesterday will never be the future
Nor will tonight; but afterwards, who knows
In what fine body I'll foresee a feature
Of her through whom my true love undergoes?

Across the vase where last week's flowers look up
Decay is complex in them; they impend
Backwards to watch you: we try to understand
How you will melt my darling, but we slip
Underneath, stagnant: or, simplified beyond
The simplification of shadows, fall asleep.

To Sydney Goodsir Smith

Dear Sydney,
    Now the time has come and gone
  When I should first have written, and the second
Has gone as well, the third, fourth, and so on,
  As many times as mathematicians reckoned
Before they found infinity, yet I've none
  The less most commendable and fecund
Intentions of inscribing to you what
Your generosity might describe as thought.

Kind thoughts, of course, but some of such a kind
  That only kindness could give them a meaning
—The odds and ends that rattle in my mind
  Without much purpose but to set it careening
In dangerous waters never yet defined
  By the hydrographers with a poetic leaning
Who wrote in Latin, Greek, Cyrillian, Medic or
Otherwise aped the charts of Yonge and Snedecor.

Halfways a young man, half already ancient
  (If years of error can make young men old)
I still discover in myself a penchant
  For telling all the worst that can be told
Of others' or my own so well-intentioned
  Activities and abstentions so I'll scold
Your laziness too and say I'm sorry not
To have received word of you—not even a blot.

Since I last saw you I've been writing sonnets,
  Some of them good, some awful. Now, they're done,

Fifty, at least, I like. The critical hornets
    Will have been kind no doubt if I'm left one
But that will do to take the sequence on its
    First stage in journeying towards the oblivion
Everything's headed for—including critics,
Sonnets and sinners, poets and paralytics.

I must confess—for me responsibility
    Seems irresponsible now. Give what one can,
One must. But since we're in the world's senility
    There's hardly anything more ridiculous than
Indulging in that sort of versatility
    Which gives it only in a verbal can
It will take centuries to open up
And, though it preserves, will not let others sup.

It is a matter of making food available
    While there remain some human minds to fill,
Defeating evils while they're still assailable,
    Not safe as dancers underneath the hill,
And finding faults before, become infallible,
    Men can no longer speak out good or ill:
This is the matter that should make us worry
And it is why I'm in this hellish hurry.

But then, of course, I'm cursed by what I've been
    And can't forget the words, and I'm not serious.
A frivolous and half-baked libertine
    I'm best ensconced, half back, in some small
        beery house
Where talk is tiny, and the custom mean.
    My critical mind is merely deleterious.
I don't attack. I simply denigrate
The things and thoughts my own words couldn't state.

[205]

Well, Sydney, there's no point in writing these
    Stupidities to you. They're best forgotten.
I go to sea on Tuesday: there the sea breeze
    May clear the clutter and make good the rotten
Glare of my thoughts. Meantime I have to wheeze
    Through the best words I can; the worst are not
      in
This letter which is signed by whom I loath
And sent to say that I still love you both.

To Norman McCaig

Dear Norman:
    This is the world's starvation centre.
    I sit with Robert Colquhoun and Robert
      McBride
Listening to letters Sydney Graham once sent or
    Barker shook down when words stuck in his side.
The frost, its brittle miracles, placenta
    Of human coldness, grinds in the fog: and wide
Arenas fill with traffic jams though traffic
Jams up my rhythm's constipated Sapphic.

'No, I shall never in the years remaining'
    Etcetera and etcetera and etcetera.
Poor Browning knew the powers, that they were
    waning
    And that, since something must be, why then
      better a
Power of barren noise than the profaning
    Silence with an anaesthetic letter, a
Sculpting where the stone remains a block,
Paintings pissed on to canvas for the shock.

So let's have noise, with that full dangerous lilting
    Milkmaids remember when the milking's done
When strands of the horizon are seen silting
    A slow obscurity down on the gold sun:
Let's have the noise of love, and the louder tilting
    Poets, political within a pun,
Make out of hate: let's put the halt in motion,
Jam on the traffic, and on nouns a notion.

We've had enough of those great ebony thoughts
    That sweat monsoons of tears most sentimental
And drown intelligence underneath the blots
    Ink weeps. This frost is honestly my placental
Link with the world outside. Transparence clots
    My windows and their frames, and from my
        lintel
There hangs, the world short-circuited by my cycle,
A dagger drawn, it's cold, a damned big icicle.

Enter. Be careful. That cold knife can rip
    Such hotheads off as do not bow before it.
Keep a cool head. It's slippery. You might trip.
    If you've a thought we'll need a place to store it.
Cold storage always. Keep a cool head and sip
    My neat liqueur; no tongue can quite adore it.
It takes a head for drink to taste this brew
Mature, mild, potent, not an ingredient new.

To Hell with all originality.
    Back to the origin, for I had liefer
Have the intelligence that makes a bird fly
    Or the old passions of a year-young heifer
Than those quaint mobs of concepts which imply
    That the done thing's the undone, smoke a reefer
Make pals with poison, sleep with everyone
And, when you can't sleep, kill a cat for fun:

Make poems out of prose, think with your senses,
    Feel with your head, (my head feels somewhat
        heavy),
Dive in the sky, discover twenty tenses
    Of that dead verb 'to be' and then a bevy

Of participles that are quite as dense as
    A neuter noun. O god, how new thoughts levy
A tax on all the actual: their Satanic
Alchemy's revelations all prove manic.

For Edwin Muir

An old man with an edge to him
In a round world that goes around
About us since it can't go on,
He deserves a little praise
As he does some love: but since
He has the small eyes of an ancient sparrow
He doesn't need a mirror's admonition
To conjure kingdoms that he lets us see.

For Josef Herman

Nothing, nothing, nothing
Can never ever happen
To this man who sits here
Some distance from the river.

His plump and portly hands
Conjure the daylight out
Of the pits' blackness and
Absorb the sun of Spain.

The Hebrides are his,
The ghetto and the city.
His loneliness is such
That children love to share it.

Companionship is his
And wise frivolities
I wonder, if you could look
Quietly into his eyes

And they laughed as confidently
As the humming wings of flies,
If it would seem to you
That you had never died.

Kiss the Girls and Make them Cry

For George Barker

The seven children and dozen books you got for your
   sins
Engender a dangerous, if perennial, emblem
Of our fleshy family, its innocence damned by your
   dream
Of a woman with words at her elbow and a hand that
   grins.
Old kings, when they had cousins, seldom lived long
Enough to make their will supreme: they were
   murdered,
As Shakespeare tells us, before they could do much
   wrong.
And the howls of the tortured monarch, are they
   what you heard?
Yes. You, George, with so many words on your head,
(Those greasy words polish away with your scalp)
Can you hear the yells of murder or the exploded dud
Cartridge the king had really to fear? Or help
The man you bandaged with a mirror when
His thankless children tried to end his reign?

In Memoriam: Keith Douglas

(for G.S.F.)

That handsome boy, the flesh encased a shadow,
A flash of darkness past us, as he rushed toward
His patriot's end: he is dead Keith Douglas,
The absurd nobility of that wise bravado.

The imprisoned shadow slumped behind his smile
Has been let loose now that a bullet's broken
Into his spirit and his strength is taken
Away from us who lack its style.

His was the grandest manner, assuming only
One axiom of glory: simplify.
He trusted God would teach him how to die
And kept his language plain and homely.

His vast gay innocence, and the sense of guilt
His final innocence fostered, gave the living
Douglas ability to go on forgiving
Himself, his killers and those he killed.

And the dead Douglas and the punctured skull
That thinks no poems and can forgive nothing?
Shadows enlarge: we, guilty of our own loathing,
Are dignified by what we kill.

The Song of the Seven Senses

My brain swims in the same blood
    As seven senses swim in,
The animal five you've thought of and
    A sense of time, and meaning.

When my blood dries, dust in the damp,
    This brain, these seven senses,
There is no knowing but their ways
    Must take four different courses:

The animal five, fish not afloat,
    Dies while the blood is drying:
The brain, left squirming on a page,
    Moulders more slowly.

But sense of time, amphibian, will
    Desert my dying body
To seek another bloodstream where
    Strange thoughts of me can flow.

As for the sense of meaning, it
    Is not at home in blood:
Should it not drown before the grave
    All seven will survive.

Memorabilium

I tell you straight the memory is
Either the best or worst of this,

The most intense, the least like what
Life seems to be and yet is not:

But most intense this memory is
Like life that lingers on to kiss

The shadows underneath the skin
Which that lamp cast, unlit for sin.

A Landscaped Room

Now that these threats
Like grey hairs
Hedge the sun's
Chubby brilliance,
Its boy's brash face
Discountenanced
By clouds and rains,
Two panes of glass
Shortsightedly
Glaze roughened stones,
The garden soil's
Moist breathing
Gathered outside.

'Keep distance out,'
The carpet cries.
A door dreams.
Walls sulk.
Warmth whispers
Threatened by mirrors.

But a discord
From overhead
Tumbles, trickles
And blackens the garden.
The greyhaired sun
Hears, as golden
Boys never can,
The patter of tears
In the deep distance.

[216]

An adult sun
Listens to trouble.
No answer is given.
The question rests.

The door crumples.
The carpet cries.
Stones return
The unbroken look
And distance sneers
At the room's two
Hollow eyes.

Another Image

Naked, stripped of her secrets, mine, tonight,
Ready and full of flesh, she is my own
Discovery or beginning or an end.
She is without the depths that shallow light
Paints on the pants, the stockings, or the breasts
Of girls who never, in their nerves, could come
Near me, and be my own. My passion rests
Beyond me, but, within her, is at home.

Tonight, sleeping the sleep of the great beasts
In a carboniferous delta, we will imagine
Another image for ourselves than ghosts
Paint dismally on every unused mind:
Naked in darkness to the last degree,
She lies too plain for any man to see.

Africa

Africa happened a long time ago.
It was merely the scent of coffee
Inhaled through thin nostrils
That made it happen to me
But at that moment it seemed to appear
On my right hand side, twenty degrees left,
And it entered my bloodstream with huge lunges
Which I couldn't shift.
The black and white were merry at once
And I couldn't agree which was which.
The white had stolen molasses from me
And the black was a bitch.
They entered, both right, and began to grapple
Until they were all on the floor.
I looked about carefully and discovered
That a corridor led to a mirror.
There black and white transplanted were
And worth emerged the victor.
I thought it sad, in many ways mad
And I hid behind the door.

The Colour Question

Is heaven the colour of the Cross?
   And what was that, I ask?
An old mahogany or a pine?
   Or cedar? Heart or bark?
Is heaven a sunlit bathing beach
   On which our cronies bask?
Or is it more what lovers know
   And therefore always dark?
     Dreams are the primary colour.

I think I have seen heaven once.
   It was late afternoon.
I dozed, and hardly half-awoke.
   I watched the firelight slant
Within the grate and on the roof
   Until I seemed to swoon
And knew there could be nothing that
   I didn't really want.
     Dreams are the primary colour.

There came a muddle, light and dark
   And each as deep as each.
I hardly knew which way to turn
   To find the firelight's glow.
I felt that I was settling down
   And sinking out of reach
Of every touch and every kiss
   And everything I know.
     Dreams are the primary colour.

And in that act of being torn
  From all that I possessed
I learned that nothing had been lost
  Nor could be lost by me
And that this strange congestion was
  Instressed and interstressed
With any affirmation I
  Had given maturity.
    Dreams are the primary colour.

My chair sagged back and I awoke.
  It was late afternoon.
I turned and carefully looked round
  At pictures on the wall,
The old settee, the gramophone
  That never played a tune,
The magazines, the firelight's glow
  That made the shadows fall.
    Dreams are the primary colour.

And as I looked I thought that I
  Had come away from heaven.
I tried and tried to remember it,
  But I was at a loss.
Nothing came back, try as I would,
  Except that I was driven
To half believe it must have been
  The colour of the Cross.
    Dreams are the primary colour.

But what that was I never learned,
  Mahogany or fir?
It could have been heart-wood of teak
  For all that I could say.

It could have been the colour of
   The spoon with which I stir
A stew that bubbles on the grate.
   It could have been field-grey.
    Dreams are the primary colour.

It could have been. . . It could have been. . .
   But it was there I know.
I heard no music and no voice
   Conjured eternity.
But it was, is, around me now
   And everywhere I go
I carry it and quarry it
   For it is part of me.
    Dreams are the primary colour.

The Negress

That tough unbounded woman gave me more
Than to the owl its feathers or its skin
To an amphibian: in her I lived within
My proper world and paused but to adore,
Surrogate to the moon. Her face was cramped,
The body heavily discarded mine
As being spun of members far too fine
For her parched darkness that no fire had damped.
Black, and the blackness glared all pale religion
Into its slack, teased out frivolities
And opened up the core whose shames are legion
To the opaqueness of the winter skies.
And yet could love them: seeing blindly love
The pranks and plots that they were symptoms of.

Skin

That sullen blackamoor with stupid eyes
Looks up at me and does not understand.
Or does he hear the backwards of my life,
That single thrush song in the sparrows' land?

Oh no, he cannot. I myself can barely
Distinguish that unmonotone from chirps;
And yet I feel in all his hollow gazing
The passionate stupidity of twerps.

He knows another ignorance from mine.
He cannot sing what ignorance it is.
Language folds backward as his steps advance.
He comes, my enemy's antithesis.

And all his questions are another answer
To what I know I cannot hope to ask.
His skin on mine presents a different problem
To what I hopefully rehearse in masque.

He is outside me, but he tunnels through
My skin of dreams and wan abilities.
He is within me and I have become
That sullen blackamoor with stupid eyes.

Sonnet I

Yes, ask me what I mean. I've had enough
Being what each of me is somewhat true
And somewhat false to, that's each other me:
The custard boy, the man, the clown, the tough,
The pale and blue-eyed, or the playful huff
I hide and seek in till he patently
Isn't a joke, the old boy and the new.
Each one means something and it's simple stuff.

Ask any of them what he wants to say.
He might bawl out, tell beads, or think you rude,
Or might explain adroitly, circumspectly
What in the world it is that moves it round.
Parcel them up together in your mind
And, if you see the meaning, say who's blind.

Sonnet II

The local ogres are against me here.
They do not like the way I brush my teeth.
My dog annoys them as it slinks beneath
Their neat defences to a pint of beer.
They cannot stand the way I stand alone
As though they weren't there, as though I knew
Their clauses, causes, didn't have a clue
And that their best case was to throw a stone.

Intellect I admire, and always have,
But this is different, this is halfway there,
And all the other half is lost as were
The herd's first sheep before he taught them love.

These people are like boats beside a pier
Who cannot journey since they cannot steer.

Sonnet III

Loquaciously as that selfish agony
Spills out its groans across your crumbling room
Inflexibly emphatic as the tomb
Silence guides towards you through the day you die.
Implacably in the right it could reply
When you howl mercy at its apron strings
That, as it takes you, you took little things,
A privileged pensioner to your vanity.
Instead of that there's lightning at your door
And silent lightnings nuzzle nearer your
Imagination's bones when they lie bare
Then ever flesh fogged in red worlds could know.
A selfish agony is the last place you
Could have expected it, yet it is so,
Or covered up in brightness worlds below
For all its stark bravado there's the skull.

Sonnet IV

The sides of tempests thicken, sprawled about
Black bits of ship that somehow still can move
As though they held together though they spout
Water through holes as numerous as pores.

They spout black water, greasy, somewhat slack,
Through holes that hold it tightly as a groove
Until the rough sea shoves it smartly back,
Into the bit of ship that keeps the stores.

Stored with the ocean then, these bits don't sink
But keep up movement though the sea moves more.
Exiled, like pieces of the land, they drink
Motion and water from the tempest's snore.
Until they sleep at last at rest among
The waves that withered them and that they'd sung.

Rock Poems

I

Hard by the quarry
And the high sky was slippery with lightning
Pantomime of midges

Hard by the hill
Like a whitewashed stook with green edges
The house hid under its hedges

II

Here among time and circumstance are many,
Are cellular crystals, constantly performing the act
   of their resurrection,
And many have lasted longer, many more fragile,
   more delicate,
Are cultures of pearl, are civilisations of rock,

And we have neither right nor duty further than any
   of these,
Knowing only what *we* know and ignorant of *their*
   knowledge.
Forgive us our folly demanding a special pleader,
The additional arrogance of an intercessor.

Are crystals still perfect though trampled, fragmented
   before our beginning.

III

Only the ruin's slow sufficient language
Seems to have time to comprehend this anguish.
How long the memories of stones may be
Stones may remember or the deepest sea
But only ruins can decipher these
Or conjugate our violent centuries.

Birdsong

The speck of protoplasm in a finch's egg,
—Watch it under its spotted shell—
It will one day be pinned upon a treetop
To curl the tresses of the straight blond breeze
With auburn musics, auspicious sunburnt notes
That are for me the triumph of the scenery.

Already, quietly, it winds temptations,
Harnesses the young blood
And bridles it with promises of discovery
To the delights which all the old ones know
Are, in success, as pointless as the breeze
Or these sharp spangles trammelling the wind's beak.

A Day-down Song

Hello, it's twilight! Put
The clock on top of straight
At thought. This moment let
Outcry go down as that
'Tick-tock' in goodness what.

And let this daylight bring
A charm to ring-a-ring
Young ghosts at creep among
Reddening harvests, and sing
Quietly to a gong.

This is the time of day
Patterns to die in I
Wonder complacently
Are not on top of me
As light longs into bye;

And each minute goes straight
As slowly a lifetime that
I watch accumulate
Reforms me over of yet
With clocks to let it at.

Images

I

There must be voices! I have heard the hour
When bats are loose, peroxide blondes in power,
Ring iron for everything that dies.
In the long synagogue of contraries
There must be voices. Hearts like muzzles gape.
Autumn's sharpshooters falter. Birds escape.

This prison daily pranks a new procession
Where, circus clowns in constant retrogression,
The seasons spin with painted faces, airs.

II

They meet their masters, sunrise-scented briar,
The quiet canticles of dew on fire,
And are afraid—for space holds so much sky
It might forget them as it hurries by.
They must meet their masters and begin to see
The secret care, the compassed instancy.

And only they can praise the way completely.

The Narrow Lyric

The narrow lyric gropes
Neatly between two times
And slowly on slanting ropes
I knot with a word that rhymes.
It bears me back over years,
Back to a self who sneers.

He has occasion for
Surprise, even contempt,
Whenever he reaches a door
Behind which he once dreamt.
A leak of blood just drips
From his apocalypse.

The narrow lyric joins
This time to that time when I
Thundered with eager loins
After who caught my eye.
Now, in this shibboleth,
I merely wait for death.

The Rains Came Early

The rains came early. It was autumn in
My shallow empire folded in the grass.
The swallows' flight was certain. All birds else
Sang in a splendid mimicry of dawn,
Their feathers faced by phenomenon,
Sang high as here is sorrow until dust
Brought many a silt and many an autumn pest:
Until the forest fell my boughs sang on.
And then I fell to seed, in early rain,
And all I did was done without the sun,
And did I rise I did discover bone,
And did I rise I did fall down again
My shallow empire fell to dust though I
Saw stone and strove towards shadows in the sky.

Sometimes I Meet my Dead

Sometimes I meet my dead and with a word
Like lightning in a scabbard of black sky
I answer and am quickened, overheard.
My dead approach lest I should die.
It is their way sometimes to nestle down
Or crouch like robbers or be scared and rise.
It is their way to do as would have done
Their new swift state slowed down by memories.
I do not love my dead: I do not dote,
Mourn nor obey them, but I often swear
To try by every hour remaining yet
To give them reason to forgive my share
In customary evil: and then I know
That I believe my dead just are not so.

Parting

Let me forget that I may forgive you
The enmity of this silence,
The necessity of this comfort,
The lingering of this anguish,
My incapacity to love you.

Let me forget, for I have pretended
Comprehension of what
I could not hope to reach,
Could not possess, could not
Leave and love uncomprehended.

Pretended love, pretended
Fear and passion, all,
Now all is almost ended
But forgiving and forgetting,
That is everywhere extended.

Undone For My Own Sake

As drowning in my blood, I lie awake,
As dreaming in my nature, I revert,
As doing in my fallacy, I try
As is my nature, to affirm, assert.

A company that's seriously mine
Elongates like the shadow of a snake
As it stands up to bite. And I am bit
More by the shadow than the teeth of it.

That shadow deepens blood and lets me drown,
Alters the nature I am dreaming by
And makes fallacious my assertive act
Until I am undone for my own sake.

The World is Thin

The brash collapse that starts in a boy
When he finds the world is thin.
He pulls the high skies down
To give the earth a reason.

The moon comes first, a cool
Skull of white light.
Its orbit-pitted face
Is laced with granite.

The Mars makes peace. Venus invites wisdom,
A paunchy Saturn smiles through sweet white wine.
Old Pluto splutters like an excited fiddle,
And Mercury abides.

And then the sun comes down.
Its eyes are heavy with a leaden rind.
The Milky Way begins
To gather on the ground.

The galaxies arrive, each greedy for the earth,
They congregate in deserts and on shores.
And the poor boy is painted by their light
White! He walks white through a morass of stars.

Preparation

I really must prepare myself for death.
Not now. It is too early.
But wait and in a little while
The world will stop its whirl.
Then indeed I will be ready, I will prepare.
The funeral parlour will be laid out nice.
And I'll get out of the cupboard where I'm bare,
And wreath myself in space.
And then a thousand knitted apologies
Will faster allay prudence.
I shall become
The victim of my own inimitable radiance.
And then I'll cease to die.
Who wants his death? When every window's low
And all the world
Waits, and expects, his corpse to be through?
But all these dumb heroics have an end.
It isn't mine, but that has seldom worth.
The only thing I know about is that
I really must prepare myself for death.

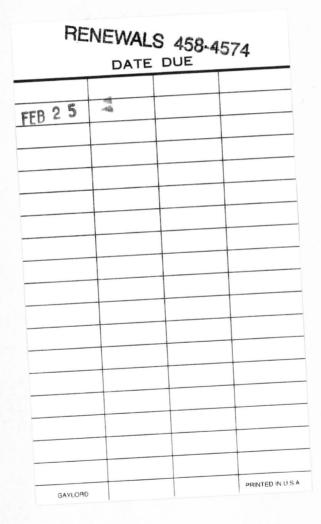